4 -

Dialectics of War

Dialectics of War

AN ESSAY IN THE SOCIAL THEORY OF TOTAL WAR AND PEACE

Martin Shaw

PLUTO PRESS

First published 1988 by Pluto Publishing Ltd
11–21 Northdown Street, London N1 9BN

Copyright © Martin Shaw 1988

Printed and bound in the United Kingdom by
Billing & Sons Ltd, Worcester

British Library Cataloguing in Publication Data

Shaw, Martin, 1947 –
   The dialectics of war : an essay in the social
   theory of war and peace.
   1. Pacifism   2. War and society
   I. Title
   303.6'6   JX1938

ISBN 0–7453–0258–0

Contents

Preface

Edward Thompson asserted, in his famous essay 'Notes on Exterminism: the last stage of civilisation'[1], that there is no dialectic in the arms race. More recently, Anthony Giddens has argued that 'no plausible "dialectical counterpart" to the progressive accumulation of military power seems to exist.'[2] Both have seen this as a basic question mark against classical socialist views of history, and indeed as raising fundamental doubts about the ability of human society to survive at all.

This book goes both further and, I hope, deeper in its challenge to received ideas. It argues that there *was* a dialectic of social change in the development of modern total war. The contradictions of warfare and society took over and distorted the conflicts arising from the relations of production which most saw as central to the direction of industrial capitalist societies. The history of all forms of socialism in this century has been bound up with the history of total war in ways which socialist theory did not anticipate and, even more lamentably, has failed to understand even after the event.

I argue, however, that the relationship of war and society has changed in the nuclear age. Militarism is not what it was: nuclear militarism does not mobilise society or require the same forms of state control as previous phases of total war.

It is true that the inner development of war itself no longer leads to radical social change. The loosening of the central state control, with the movement beyond total war, has moreover created new possibilities for free-market capitalism. This book asks the left, too, to move beyond the politics of total war, and suggests that there may be new openings for socialist and peace politics in the changed relationships of warfare and society. But these will only be grasped if war is seen as the central problem which it is.

This is an essay in theory, touching on many areas in a general way: history of ideas, history of war, socialism and peace politics. Those whose interests are more narrowly in one of these areas may find the ideas in need of further development. I hope, though, that bringing them together helps us to ask questions and begin new arguments. This, above all, is the aim of this book.

Martin Shaw
Hull, July 1987

Acknowledgements

I have learnt much from co-workers of many kinds – from my friends in the peace movement, especially in European Nuclear Disarmament, which is undoubtedly its intellectual powerhouse; from political comrades on the left, who have helped, often unwittingly, to stimulate my unorthodox ideas; and especially from the small band of historically minded sociologists who have begun to work seriously on problems of war and society. I mention none of them by name because this is very much an individual enterprise, and no one else is responsible for my simplifications or mistakes. Specific intellectual debts are, I hope, acknowledged in the text and notes.

More practically, I must thank colleagues and students at Hull who have not only tolerated but encouraged my interests at a time when institutional pressures are all for concentration of effort in established fields. Even more practically, I must thank Melanie Bucknell, Stella Rhind and, last but not least, Pat Wilkinson, who have all typed parts of the text.

Special thanks must go to Richard Kuper, founder of Pluto Press, with whom I first discussed this book back in 1981, for his encouragement. His patience with me was overtaken by the crisis of Pluto, which in turn led to further delays in publication. I must also thank those at Allison and Busby who pushed the project forward, and Pluto Publishing Ltd who have finally brought it out.

My deepest thanks go to my children, Katy, Thomas and Isabel, who have encouraged me and made it all worth while in ways they may not always understand. This book is dedicated to my parents, Roy and Gwen Shaw, to whom I owe much more than I have often understood.

1
Critique of Sociology and Military Theory

The fear of war hangs over society. This is almost literally true, for it is not the invader in the streets but the warhead exploding on us which dominates our nightmares. The descent of the intercontinental missile is a symbol of the external character of war: a danger which appears from completely outside the everyday social relations in which most people live, confronting them with absolute obliteration. This sort of war seems far removed from society, even from the activities of the considerable part of society professionally concerned with war, that is the armed forces and armaments workers. They are too reassuringly human, sharing as individuals the mundane economic troubles and social anxieties of their fellow citizens, to fully represent the awfulness of the threat to life on earth.

Yet the existence of these social groups reminds us that war is something which is prepared within society. Just as an immense concentration of human activity in the Soviet Union produces the missiles which could destroy us, so a comparable social organisation here produces similar missiles aimed at them. Western democratic societies, especially in Europe, may be among the least overtly militaristic which civilisation has produced, but we harbour the most murderous weapons ever created, and we devote the greatest resources ever provided by any society, outside actual war, to producing and maintaining them. The isolation of missile bases in the countryside, away from centres of population, is another physical symbol of the disjunction of nuclear militarism from our urban-industrial world. But it is a disjunction which is more apparent than real, since the nuclear weapons-systems originate in that society and, if they are used, will return to it with a most terrible vengeance.

Nevertheless the role of war, and war-preparation, in the modern world presents us with an essential paradox. How is it that a society which has created such potential for human liberation – in technology, human cooperation, and ideas – can produce at the same time and with the same means such appalling danger? The conflict of these two sides of our society must ultimately be resolved, in practice as well as in theory. However obvious this point is from a simple human point of view, it has not proved easy for thinkers to grapple with, any more than it has been easy to overcome the conflict in the real social and political world. Most thinkers about society have not been able to grasp the huge problem which war poses for our understanding of society in general: they have marginalised it, treated it as exceptional, abnormal, etc. Most thinkers about war, on the other hand, have tended to treat it as if it were a self-contained process, certainly depending on society for its resources, but ultimately operating according to its own laws. Although the more intelligent of them have recognised the implications of modern warfare for society, they have generally dealt with them much too obliquely, for fear perhaps that these implications would simply topple the whole edifice of military thought and practice.

The problem of war and society can therefore be seen as a dilemma, the horns of which have been tackled separately by social and military theory, but the heart of which has rarely been exposed. The aim of this book is to confront this dual problem, of how society has changed war and how war has changed society, as a unity. One writes 'has changed' because it is important to understand the problem historically, to see the processes which have created the present situation. But it is this problem, the danger of nuclear war in our time and the social institutions which sustain that danger while being distorted by it, which gives the argument its coherence and direction.

This book takes its premises from both social and strategic thought, while criticising both. On the one hand, it argues, with such social theory as has considered war, that war must be seen as a social activity related to the whole complex of social life and organisation. On the other, it agrees with strategic writing that war must be seen as a very unique social activity, with its own character and logic which cannot be reduced to any ordinary social dynamic. The relationship of war and society is portrayed as one of constant tension. It is argued that there are dialectics of war and society which, while they grow out of other social contradictions, fundamentally alter the social process as a whole. The dialectics of war not only threaten to displace the dialectic of social change which has been considered by a whole tradition of social analysis: they posit the danger of a fundamentally different end to human history. If we are to avoid this end, we need to understand the processes which are producing it, and to grasp the contradictions which offer some rational basis for optimism about the outcome.

This chapter is devoted to exploring this theoretical issue: first by a discussion of how social science has failed to grapple with the nature of war itself, and second by a critique of strategic theory, which is more interesting in its treatment of this problem, but has generally abstracted it too much from its socio-historical context.[1] In conclusion, a proposal will be made as to how the relationships between war and society should be understood in general terms. This will lay the foundation for the historical treatment in the middle chapters, which discuss how the tension of war and society has worked through the nineteenth and twentieth centuries, and for the final chapter which focusses again on the politics of war and peace in the nuclear age.

The failure of social theory

For virtually all schools of social thought, wars are exceptional phases of social life, abnormal phenomena which interrupt the fundamental social patterns. On this point there is no serious disagreement between, say, a functionalist sociologist like Talcott Parsons, for whom society is essentially consensual and harmonious, and a Marxist theorist of modes of exploitation and class struggle. War is as much a disturbance of the ordinary pattern of capitalist development and class conflict as it is of the self-equilibriating social system.

Warfare is recognised as a social activity. Most social theorists would accept the anthropological arguments that war, while near-universal, is nonetheless a social rather than a biological or psychological product. Some sorts of warmaking in 'primitive' societies are indeed so ritualised and minimally violent that they are readily accommodated under the rubric of routine social life.[2] Ritualisation, routinisation and regulation are also recognised to be part of the process of war-preparation and even of war-fighting right up to the present day. The rituals of tribal warfare are echoed in the medieval codes of chivalry and even in the arcane pursuit of war-limitation by nuclear strategists.[3] Routinisation is evident in the bureaucratisation of warfare: military institutions are models or reflections, according to one's analysis, of the general form of social organisation in our time. Regulation, although woefully inadequate to the goals of preventing or controlling war, is subscribed to in principle by all states. It is evident in the plethora of international laws, conventions and institutions, although these are of dubious practical value.

Despite a wide acceptance of the social character of war, it is equally widely excluded from the basic models of modern society which are on offer in social science. The concept of 'industrial society' which has informed mainstream sociology from Saint-Simon, Comte and Durkheim onwards was defined by contrast with the military hierarchy of feudal-agrarian society. It was proposed by Comte, for example, in the belief that a rational, scientific social organisation of labour – the basic sense of 'industry' – must imply peace. It has long since been proven that this optimism was utterly misplaced:[4] but the concept of 'industrial society' has survived, minus the assertion of pacificism, as a *de facto* model of a warless society. Sample any sociological textbook and you will look in vain for a discussion of war among the institutions of industrialism.[5] Where early nineteenth-century theory explained war away (with superficial historical justification, as it turned out, since the end of the Napoleonic Wars ushered in a century without general conflicts), late twentieth-century theory, which ought to confront a war-ridden century, largely ignores the uncomfortable facts.

The model of 'capitalism' derived from Marx offers no more direct, basic recognition of war than that of 'industrial society'. Marx too assumed – indeed articulated – the nineteenth-century separation of civil society and the state. The Marxist theoretical edifice was built on the autonomy of the mode of production from the state: everything to do with the state, international relations, even international trade, was abstracted from Marx's basic model. Capitalism was the 'pure' mode of production *par excellence*: however sullied by the historical survival of less pure modes, it was tending towards a direct social conflict between labour and capital. Change would arise from the dialectic of class struggle, springing from the contradictions of forces and relations of production in the capitalist mode. War was seen by Marx as very much a secondary phenomenon, determined perhaps by the economic base (in ways which we shall discuss later), but providing little more than an external influence on social development. Later Marxism confronted the twentieth-century experience of war by adapting the model, to theorise about the state, imperialism and nationalism. These code words have entered the wider sociological parlance, generally permitting their users to skirt round the problem of war by examining the wider economic, political and ideological relations: rarely the social process of war itself. The classical Marxist tradition on this point has been reconstructed in a narrowly orthodox way. Lenin's theoretical conservatism, which separated imperialism and the state, has become the focal point of subsequent debate, rather than Bukharin's more radical model which saw these as fused under the impact of world war.[6]

Where the main body of social science recognises the problem of war, it invariably translates it into one of 'militarism'. The distinction between war, the actual conflict, and militarism, the preparation and ideology of war, is a crucial one, without which there can be no understanding of the relationship between the two. War-preparation is, in appearance, an 'ordinary' social activity, integrated institutionally into all the structures of society – economic, political and cultural. It can, it seems, be analysed in these terms, without reference to its ultimate ends. War itself, on the other hand, is a wholly exceptional, abnormal affair, at best an intrusion into the social structure which may temporarily suspend its usual workings. Seen in this way, it is no surprise that while social science has had some thoughts on militarism, which can be linked to capitalism, imperialism, nationalism and the state, it has had all too few on war. It has been reluctant to admit that at the heart of the social institutions of contemporary capitalism lurks a destructive potential of the kind which modern warfare represents. It is as if a principle alien to social-scientific thinking threatens to distort the whole development of society: not just at some future date when the whole structure is vaporised, but now as the processes of war-preparation insinuate themselves into social life.

The heart of this problem is the premise of rationality. Mainstream social science has been built on an axiom that people will seek to fit means to ends: what does not satisfy this model is a residue of the traditional, the sentimental, in the end the 'irrational'. This idea dominates economics, politics and sociology. When formulated, as for example by Max Weber, it has been criticised in a number of ways: the irrationality of the choice of ends; the effect of irrational factors on the choice of means; and (relevant to our discussion) the irrational effects of conflicts betweeen opposing 'rational' actions.[7] But the criticisms have hardly upset the persistence of the basic assumption, which has simply been qualified or redefined, for example by Marxists for whom the agents of rational action are primarily classes, and its ends determined by class interests.

The problem is that war is seen by social science as a means, governed by ends which are determined in economic, social and political life. But war, as a means, has unique characteristics, which are becoming more and more contradictory to the ends for which it might be waged; and it has its own logic and rationality which can impose themselves on society. War appears not only to be escaping from the control of rational social interests, but to be taking society with it. The attempt to treat war, or the preparation for it within society, under the rubric of social rationality reaches a point where it breaks down under the recognition of what war has really become.

The limits of strategic thought

Strategic thought might appear to be dominated by the same assumption of rationality. After all, it was Clausewitz who wrote: 'War is nothing but the continuation of policy by other means' – an idea which endeared him to Lenin and others in the Marxist tradition. Certainly, modern strategic thought is based on the belief that armed force can be an effective instrument of political policy, and fears, above all, the argument that this is no longer true in the nuclear age.

Clausewitz himself provides us with the basis for criticising this notion. War's function as an instrument of policy was only one element, alongside primordial violence and the play of chance: together these composed the 'remarkable trinity' in his definition. The essence of war as a means was the actual process of *fighting*, and all the other activities of war – the business of war-preparation, which has become such an industry in our day – were devoted to this end. In fighting, the destruction of the enemy's force was the primary goal, best achieved in a single great battle or 'slaughter'.[8]

Clausewitz was at great pains to emphasise this 'destructive principle' of warfare. It constituted his view of the very nature of war: it was 'an act of force', and there is *no logical limit to an act of force*.[9] The resort to force – or, more precisely, to violence, or indeed to killing, the ultimate destructive action of human beings against each other – was a total commitment. Once two powers were set in violent motion against each other, there was no limit until one had destroyed the other's capacity for resistance, and subordinated it to its will.

War was, of its nature, total and absolute: this was Clausewitz's crucial insight, which has caused so many problems for modern strategic theory. True, it was greatly qualified, and rightly so. Clausewitz stands out in strategic thinking partly for the acuteness of his social and historical awareness. He wished to highlight how it was that the involvement of the people, as a result of the French Revolution, had intensified military conflicts, compared to the much more limited affairs of the eighteenth century. He emphasised, on the other hand, that war was never a self-contained activity, and that it was restricted by the circumstances in which it was fought. In his famous concept of 'friction' he crystallised the idea that, while war might *tend towards* the total, there were in practice all sorts of constraints on this tendency (geographical, technical, logistic). Real war always fell short of the 'ideal' of a total contest of force.

Friction, as much as the totalising tendency of force, was something inherent in war itself. But it clearly depended greatly on the general socioeconomic, technological and political conditions of warfare. This is something we can see all the more clearly now that technology has overcome so many of the sources of friction in previous wars. As Michael Howard points out, Clausewitz prophetically envisaged a situation in which friction was eliminated:

If war consisted of one decisive act, or a set of simultaneous decisions, preparations would tend towards totality, because no omission could ever be rectified. The sole criterion for preparations which the world of reality would provide would be the measures taken by the adversary, so far as they are known; the rest would once more be reduced to abstract calculations.[10]

Howard rightly comments that this is 'a depressingly accurate description of contemporary nuclear strategy . . . all [the] internal constraints on "absolute war" have been removed and its complete realisation has for the first time become a practical possibility'.[11]

Clearly, immense social changes lie behind this achievement of the potential for absolute war. The development of modern industrial capitalism, state systems, technology: these are the preconditions. But such sociological explanation should not detract from the central point. War has reached in theory, if not yet in practice, the inner limit which Clausewitz so brilliantly defined for it: the total and instantaneous destruction of the 'enemy' (which becomes, of course, mutual destruction). In reaching this limit, war also negates itself. If there are no longer internal constraints, and war becomes absolute destruction, it becomes invalid as a means of policy. Discriminating ends require discriminating means.

Modern strategic thought clearly recognises the dangers that, as war approaches this inner limit, military force becomes unusable. Much of modern strategy can be seen as an attempt to avoid redundancy. Essentially it has taken two forms: the attempt to rehabilitate strategy first as a means of war-avoidance rather than war-fighting and, second, by envisaging limited wars short of total nuclear war. Both these responses recognise the theoretical limit of all-out nuclear war: the first by accepting it, and hence displacing the goal of military preparation from war itself to 'deterrence'; the second by recoiling from it to levels at which policy goals and friction become meaningful again. Both these responses, which in practice tend to overlap, are in the end evasions of, rather than solutions to, the crisis of war.

This is most obvious in the case of the 'deterrence' response. On one level, of course, deterrence *is* rational: states are indeed inhibited by the awesome destructive power with which they face each other. For so long as this is the case, deterrence may 'work'. But on another level, the concept is patent nonsense, and at its worst sheer political sophistry. There can be no general distinction between deterrence and warfighting, since the enemy is only deterred if it believes in our willingness to use our weapons. The credibility of the 'deterrent' is as much a matter of will as of technical capacity, as the development of strategy and weaponry has shown in the past. The crisis of the crude deterrence of 'mutually assured destruction' was precisely that because of the undoubted destructive capacity of strategic missiles, willingness to use them was dubious. The logic of deterrence demanded more limited weaponry, because it was more credible that this would be used. This development – the US strategy of 'flexible response' and the corresponding gradations of strategic, intermediate and battlefield nuclear weapons – was not a transition from 'deterrence' to 'warfighting'. It was, rather, a demonstration that warfighting was always inherent in deterrence: that they are two sides of the same 'strategy'. It was also a demonstration that the business of strategy cannot seriously be redefined as one of war-avoidance.

Concepts of 'limited war' are sometimes advanced as part of a 'deterrence' posture, but also – more honestly – with some indication of a belief that such wars can actually be fought. In one sense this is obviusly true: there is still considerable scope for conventional wars in the Third World, both between local states and between such states and the Northern powers. But this 'space' for war expresses the relative backwardness of the Third World, and its incomplete incorporation into the superpower conflict. And while militarisation is in one sense increasing the scope for war, in a more general perspective the limits of war are appearing: first because of the nuclearisation of the Third World, and secondly because of the linkages between local and superpower conflict. Although local conflicts may be fought, and *may* in fact remain limited, it is becoming less possible to say categorically that they will be. The risks are rapidly increasing.

The real argument about limited war concerns direct conflict between the superpowers. Two sorts of limitation can be envisaged, by geography and weaponry, although in practice the limitations are likely to coincide. In either case, limitation will depend not just on arbitrary attempts to restrict the 'damage' of war, but on an understanding or convention of war as a form of conflict resolution.[12] No such understanding has been successfully proposed, still less agreed, between the superpowers. It seems preposterous to think that it could be: that given the immense destructiveness of even a conventional war in Europe, let alone a limited nuclear exchange, such a war could be restricted to preconceived levels of response by rational political decision. It is historically true that even the wars which were most obviously limited, by political circumstances and goals as well as weaponry, have tended to surpass the limits initially foreseen for them. It is impossible to believe that such a global confrontation between over-armed powers, into the avoidance of which so much has been invested, could ever be restricted if it should take place. Even if theoretically conceivable, this would be unlikely in practice, especially now that nuclear technology has created the conditions – and hence also the necessity – for a 'disarming first strike'. Escalation, which is virtually a law of war, would very probably turn out to be instantaneous, not gradual.

The social dialectics of war

Neither the deterrent nor the limited-war versions of strategic theory can divert attention from the main issue: that the *means of war have outstripped any rational use for them*. The problem with strategic theory, however, is that even when this conclusion is reached, it can offer us no way out except to prove the finality of the outcome in the actual use of nuclear weapons. The dialectic of war, considered in isolation, simply comes to a self-negating full stop. War can only be abolished, in these purely military terms, when nuclear immolation removes the means and agents of war from the face of the earth. And there must remain the suspicion that even this will not be final: that in the twilight world of the 'aftermath', the brutalised survivors will mock strategic theory with an internecine struggle for survival.

To pose the matter at all constructively we must re-integrate military theory with social thought. As the more historically minded strategic writers have understood – but the nuclear planners must needs forget – war has developed in the context of society, as one social activity among many. War can only be understood in the context of the totality of social relations. The idealised dialectic of military theory, which has expressed the active (in reality, destructive) inner character of war, needs to be transformed by a materialist social history which can show how war has arisen from and returns to society.

Strategic theory, even at its most sociological, has generally seen these relations – society–war–society – in terms that are too linear. In explaining that war expresses social purposes, and necessarily affects society, the strategist may too easily conclude that society must be incorporated into the battlefield. Indeed this doctrine is sometimes advanced by revolutionaries, who wish war to be a social struggle rather than a narrowly professional military activity. When formulated as a general proposition, however, the notion that war must involve 'an invasion of the fabric of the opponent's social order' (as one recent academic strategist has suggested)[13] assumes frightening overtones in the nuclear age. If society is indeed the battlefield, then society may simply be destroyed when technology makes this feasible. A sociological 'translation' of strategic theory is not enough: its only virtue is to clarify the social consequences of military concepts.

What is required is an altogether more dialectical concept

of the relations between war and society, which understands the contradictory nature of this relationship, as of society itself. War does not express the common purposes of 'society' as a whole, but arises out of particular relationships and institutions in society. Warfare has been, almost continuously in known history, a major part of the development of social conflict and contradictions. Anthropologists suggest that war was a main cause (and effect) – if not the only one – of the formation of social classes and states.[14] In large scale historical civilisations, warmaking has invariably been a core function of privileged social groups and state institutions. A dialectic of military expansion and the constant need for slaves governed the rise and fall of the Roman Empire.[15] The feudal social hierarchy of medieval Europe was closely defined by military obligations. In most pre-modern societies, the linkages of warfare and the socio-economic order are clearly defined, expressed in the dominant ideology and immediately recognised by the historian.

Only in early industrial capitalist societies is there an apparent separation, not just of warmaking, but of the entire range of state activities and institutions, from the mode of economic life. Production, as Marx argued, was initially freed from the extra-economic constraints of feudal society. For the first time, it became relatively pure commodity production, production of exchange values rather than (directly) of use values. Warfare was no longer one of the purposes of socio-economic activity, but a purpose of the highly distinct sphere of political life. The 'optimistic theory of industrial capitalism' (as Mann calls it)[16] incorrectly concluded from this institutional separation that warfare was a historical residue, unlikely to coexist for long with industrialism. The Marxist theory, more realistically, drew attention to the social linkages between the differentiated spheres of production and the state. Marxist theorists have argued that the class which owns the means of production thereby rules politically as well; or, in a more sophisticated version, that the nature of competitive capitals concerned with production of exchange values *implies* that the capitalists must constitute themselves as a class in a distinct political sphere, in order to carry out those necessary social tasks which they cannot carry out as individual capitals. Warfare is, of course, one such task, although why it remained 'necessary' in industrial capitalist society is a question which Marxist theory has hardly answered. In general, it has seen war as an extension of the competitive struggle between capitals: but the question of why the struggle between capitals takes the form of war between states requires an analysis of the system of territorial states. This system pre-dated capitalism, although of course it has been modified by it.[17]

The territorial aspect of the state, so fundamental to its very constitution, as non-Marxist definitions have suggested, is often neglected in the attempt to link the state to the internal class division of national societies. This external side of the state's functioning, connected to its role in an international system of states, is an essential feature in any attempt to link industrial capitalism and warfare. It is not possible to argue simply that capitalism itself requires warfare. It is possible to argue that capitalism historically has presupposed a system of nation-states, in which warfare is the ultimate form of conflict. Capitalism has greatly altered both the state system and warfare; and, at the same time, that the workings of the state system, and especially warfare, have fundamentally affected the nature, workings and forms of capitalism. Whether capitalism, considered from the standpoint of pure theory, requires either a state-system or war, is in this sense irrelevant: 'capitalism' is a historical abstraction from a world society structured by a system of states and warfare.

Mary Kaldor has suggested we can analyse the 'mode of warfare' in society as something analogous, but never reducible, to the mode of production. Warfare is a social activity which may have a role in terms of the socio-economic and political systems, but which has its own specific character and ends. The 'mode of warfare' should be distinguished from the 'role of warfare'. Using Clausewitz's suggestion – which appealed to Marx and Engels – that battle is to war what cash payment is to commodity exchange, Kaldor regards warfare as a rational, goal-oriented social activity loosely comparable to the system of production for profit. The comparison is limited, however, in quite crucial ways. First, battle – actual war as opposed to war-preparation – occurs so much less frequently than cash payment. Commodity values are realised thousands of times per second: military values may be untested for decades. Kaldor considers that this leads to considerable distortion of the mode of warfare, above all in the nuclear age when the use of weapons becomes self-defeating. Secondly, the mode of warfare can never reproduce itself, but is always parasitic on the mode of production. However much war and war-preparation may be carried on for their own ends, they depend on the mode of production for their resources. 'Because armaments do not re-enter the production process, the entire cost of armaments – cost of production plus mark-up – represents a deduction from surplus-value earned elsewhere in the economy'. War is therefore an 'a priori burden on and potential interruption to the process of capitalist accumulation. This tension between warfare and capitalism explodes periodically in war.'[18]

By contrast, then, with Marxists, who see warfare as necessary – almost 'functional' – for capitalism, Kaldor sees its distinct logic as a problem for capitalist accumulation. The enormous demands of the mode of warfare, in the context of a permanent arms race, distort the economy and accentuate crisis. The absence of actual war makes the mode of warfare ever more artificial, overblown and rigid, which increases the pressure for war simply to test the military plans: and yet war as a means is so obviously self-defeating. No sectors of capital can actually have a rational interest in nuclear war: some may pursue war-avoidance to the point of becoming allies of peace movements, suggests Kaldor, although she still seems uncertain of this.[19]

The dialectic of war is therefore seen, at its simplest, as leading to an opposition between war and society. War grows out of society, feeds upon the enormous growth of productive resources brought about by industrial capitalism, and will ultimately destroy not only that particular system but every form of human society. But as I have already suggested, the simple terms, 'war and society', or even 'war and capitalism' must be broken down. Each term in these pairs is highly complex: the very concept of an opposition between the two terms is increasingly misleading. While war appears to be a relatively discrete social activity, apart from society, imposing its requirements on the socio-economic system, in reality the two are closely integrated. To theorise about the 'mode of warfare' as distinct from the 'mode of production' may be necessary, in order to establish the specific requirements of warfare by contrast with those of commodity production. But to take this analytical distinction for a separation in reality is mistaken. There is no more than a partial disjunction between the two, since society (and specifically production) has been incorporated into warfare, and correspondingly warfare into society (and production). However much the requirements of warfare (in the abstract) may appear to conflict with those of production (in the abstract), in reality the tension to which Kaldor refers is muffled.

The dialectic of war and society should not therefore be seen in terms of such a simple opposition. The integration of the two means that we must modify the terms: we are talking about the role of *socialised* warfare in a *militarised* economy and society. We can no more understand the contradictions of society outside its military frame than we can those of warfare apart from its insertion in society. The integration is neither perfect nor complete, but it is fundamental to both.

The solution to the dilemmas of military theory is only to be found when this is recognised. The theoretical limit of nuclear war cannot be evaded with the deterrent or limited-war options; but neither can we wait for nuclear weapons to achieve the self-negation of warfare. The answer to the problems is to recognise that 'friction', virtually eliminated from the actual fighting of wars by the achievement of the capability for instantaneous total immolation, has been transferred back into war-preparation. The very elimination of friction from warfighting increases the friction affecting war preparation. This is true in two senses. First, the unlimited-ness of nuclear war inhibits governments both directly – in that they recognise the self-defeating nature of it – and indirectly, in that the catastrophic outcome for society creates popular pressure against war. Secondly, the nature of the economic and technical resources required for the arms race at its limit creates a new form of friction. A tension with the requirements of civilian production inhibits all but the most powerful states from full participation in it, and creates econo-mic contradictions in the military efforts of all states, even the superpowers.

Of course, these constraints on war-preparation, and on the conversion of war-preparation into warfighting, are not abso-lute. Understood only in the military sense, as 'friction', they offer no solutions, only a delay. It is only if forces exist in society which are capable of understanding the limits to war, and of acting to prevent it, that answers can be found. There is no solution in continuing to ask: How can wars continue to be fought? but only in asking: How can we create the conditions in which they will never be fought again?

At this point, it is obvious that military theory must give way to social theory, but only to a social theory which has recog-nised the immense impact of the military problem in society. Simply to identify the 'ordinary' socio-economic contradic-tions is not enough: we must examine how war and militarism have permeated the structure and processes of society, including the forces and movements often seen as offering solutions. The integration of warmaking and socio-economic development has long since passed the point at which war can be considered an 'extraneous' factor. Unless we are able to understand how war has moulded society in the twentieth century, we shall be unable even to glimpse the possibility of a solution to the problem which war now poses.

In this century, the spectre of military totalitarianism has frequently haunted society. The prospect of a ruthless, totally

manipulative regime, bent externally on military expansion
and internally on political repression, has seemed the greatest
danger and evil of our time. Because Western – and even
Communist – states are some way from this model (and they
manifestly are), because *1984* was not realised in 1984, the real
role of militarism in our society has often been under-
emphasised. The absence of the most overt forms of militarism belies the role of a subtler form. It can be shown, I
believe, that there are general and long-term tendencies
transforming industrial society as a consequence of its mode
of warfare. The nature of these tendencies and the different
forms they take is the subject of the greater part of this book;
but first it is necessary to discuss how warfare itself was
transformed by industrial capitalism.

2
Military Industrialism and the Phases of Total War

There is an emerging consensus that the old debate over whether capitalist industrialism is 'inherently' pacific or militarist is simply beside the point. According to Mann, it is neither, but there exists a contingent historical association between capitalism and war: simply because of its technical progress, capitalism has vastly increased the dangers of war.[1] According to Kaldor, as we have seen, although the mode of warfare should be seen as distinct from capitalism, the tension between the two is crucial. E.P. Thompson goes so far as to suggest that the application of industrial technology to warfare has ultimately produced a new social form, dominated by a nuclear arms race which is leading to total annihilation: 'exterminism'.[2]

The problem, it seems, is not whether to transcend the traditional sociological and Marxist debate, but how, precisely, to take the argument further. Part of the answer may be provided by the rethinking of the theory of the state which has been going on on both sides of the Atlantic. The Marxist debate, initiated by Ralph Miliband in *The State in Capitalist Society*, was carried forward in the 1970s, first in structuralist arguments about 'relative autonomy', and secondly in the state-derivationist school's attempt to locate the state within 'the logic of capital'.[3] In the 1980s, however, both the theoretical assumptions and the abstract methodology of this debate have come under sustained attack from a new group of 'institutional' theorists committed to historical-sociological research. Interestingly, a key text of this new wave, Theda Skocpol's *States and Social Revolutions*, introduced war as a key context of state-formation and revolutionary crisis. The subsequent development of the position, however, has not taken this particular aspect any further, concentrating on establishing a state-centred social theory without any special attention to war.[4] Anthony Giddens has provided an impressive historical reconstruction of state theory in which war plays a major part, but his concern is to explain the state, not war. On the other hand, Miliband has attempted to reconcile Skocpol's position with a Marxist account, in proposing a 'partnership' of state and capital.[5] But this seems an unsatisfactory compromise, which does justice neither to the powerful logic of capitalism whose effects Marxists have discussed, nor to the force of state interests argued by their critics. It is doubtful if their reciprocal historical dynamic can be expressed in a single formula; what is required is a recognition of the tensions between the requirements of capitalist industrialism and of state power, and their historically shifting balance.

A state-centred social theory, especially when it makes use of war to explain state development (as in some of Skocpol's and Giddens' work), obviously takes us closer to a theory of war and society than a mode of production-centred theory. But it is not the same thing as a social theory of war, since it will not necessarily explain how warfare has become a central determinant of social and political relations. In fact, what we need is a *war-centred* social theory. The aim of this chapter is to begin to supply some of the concepts which are necessary for this. The most useful sources are not the debates in social theory, but the more theoretically aware historical analyses of war that have been produced in recent years.

Although clearly war held a central place in many pre-industrial societies, industrialism is both so different from previous forms, and so widely seen as not inherently militaristic, that we need to start by asking how war has become central to this particular sort of society. Even to pose the question in this way could be said to accept, too easily, the assumption that the two can originally be separated, and beg the question of how real this separation ever was. It can be argued that the emergence of a competitive state-system, with frequent inter-state warfare, helped to stimulate capitalism in Europe, while the lack of both inhibited such development in other civilisations. It can also be argued, more specifically, that industrialisation was speeded up and its direction shaped by war – and, in particular, that the Napoleonic Wars had this effect on the classical 'Industrial Revolution' in Britain.[6]

The autonomy of industrial capitalism from warfare (we need to reverse the usual formula) was therefore quite relative even in its formative period. What is true, however, is that, by comparison with later historical developments, the early effects of industrialisation on warfare were minimal at this stage, and that the impact of warfare on society, although considerable, was of a different order from that which industrialised warfare was later to make. It is the great expansion of the role of war with which this chapter is concerned.

Industrialised warfare and politicised economies

McNeill dates the industrialisation of warfare from about 1840. The origins of total war are, however, earlier than this. The Revolutionary and Napoleonic wars represent a primitive model: a political, ideological and military-organisational form, although without the technical and economic basis of industrialised warfare. Population growth, resulting from agricultural improvements and the beginnings of industrialis-ation, supplied the demographic basis for mass armies: the French Revolution provided the more important elements of mass participation, citizenship, and nationalist fervour. The *levée en masse* which produced the revolutionary army of 1793 was 'an attempt to mobilise not just a mass army in a hurry but, behind it, a whole politicised population'.[7] Revolutionary nationalism motivated what was at first a people's army, although later the ideology was adapted to Napoleon's imperial ambitions.

According to Best, the Republic from 1793-4 was a 'society taken totally to war, with, for a while, price-controls and the requisitioning of labour, products and property, to a degree unprecedented and unmatched until the Second World War'.[8] Although at a primitive, labour-intensive level, Republican France under the Terror was a war-economy of a recognisably modern kind, a 'military State ... to such an extent that its turning into a military dictatorship marked the end of a logical road'.[9]

This model of 'total war' – whose revolutionary origins are of no small interest – impressed the Prussian professional soldiers who were pitted against it, and left its mark on military theory in the work of Clausewitz. But, for a century after 1814, there was no large-scale repetition of the experience, at least not in Europe, and warfare seemed once again to resemble the more limited rivalry of the eighteenth century. The most important exception was the American Civil War, in which once again mass armies were pitted against each other in years of battle, with the societies of North and South mobilised behind them. In the half-century after the close of the Napoleonic Wars, however, industrial technology had been applied to weapons, transport and communications. Mass production of guns, railways as means of moving large numbers of men, telegraphic communications: these made the Civil War 'the first full-fledged example of an industrialised war', even if this was only recognised in Europe in the bitter light of 1914-18.[10]

Industrialisation of warfare proceeded apace from the mid-nineteenth century until the full demonstration of its potential in the First World War. Technical change in land armaments, although 'radical enough measured against older standards, was modest only by comparison to the galloping transformation in naval armaments'.[11] Massive warship building programmes, beginning in Britain and France in the 1880s, were emulated in Germany and the United States in the 1890s. The scale and complexity of the new ships – and even

more of entire ship-building programmes – altered the relationship between the producers and the procurers of arms.
What McNeill calls 'command technology', in which market
relations were replaced by the design of new weaponry to
order, became dominant in the 30 years before 1914. Growing
'like a cancer within the tissues of the world's market economy',[12] naval construction created a new sector within first the
British and then other leading national economies. The big
arms firms were closely tied to their naval and political
patrons, and 'quickly evolved into vast bureaucratic structures
of quasi-public character'.[13] They were often seen by liberal
and Marxist critics as private profit-seekers whose greed was
responsible for the proliferation of arms. In reality, a sector of
capital was growing because of its dependence on state militarism and the ambitions of both civil and military
bureaucracies.[14]

As perceptive a military writer as Engels could see the state
as loser in the naval arms race and make the amazingly
optimistic comment that 'the warship is being developed to a
pitch of perfection which is making it both outrageously costly
and unusable in war'.[15] This description illustrates the inadequacy of social theory which treats war-preparation, and even
more war itself, according to 'ordinary' (i.e. market-derived,
capitalist) economic criteria. Although there must always be a
compromise between military and non-military forms of economic activity, and even more of state expenditure, the rise of
large-scale military industry is the rise of an economic sector
which is autonomous from the market and the logic of capital.
The profits of private arms firms are ultimately dependent on
the state's military purposes and on how its bureaucracies
perceive its needs. In war, the state's purposes transcend
ordinary accounting: in the twentieth century, it has become
quite normal for states to risk not only their most costly
military investments, but their whole economies and peoples.

The development of the military-industrial sector thus
introduced an alternative principle – the military requirements of the state – into the capitalist market economy. From

factors. Attacks on economic targets – not only merchant shipping but, with the development of aerial warfare, factories and dockyards – were legitimate; civilian deaths and hardship, if not actively promoted in the manner of the Second World War, could be seen as contributing to strategic goals. Civilian deaths, although still small in relation to those of combatants, were on an unprecedented scale, and many resulted directly from more indiscriminate forms of warfare by submarine, artillery and air attacks.

Taken overall, therefore, there was still a distinction between civilian and military participation in war, but it was beginning to break down. Society was incorporated into war on the supply side, as a distinct 'home front' concerned with economic and political problems rather than as a military battlefield. Especially for Britain and (in its brief participation) the USA, which were not invaded or fought over, this distinction was fairly clear, although the social effects of the human damage in the trenches were far-reaching. Equally, the distinction between civil and war economies, although far from clear in practice in the war period, in general remained, and wartime controls were seen as 'abnormal'. Attempts to adapt the war model of economic organisation to the social problems of peace were too weak to withstand the post-war re-emergence of the inherent problems of the capitalist market economy.[19]

Nevertheless, neither states nor societies reverted to their pre-1914 condition. The world before the war vanished – indeed one side of it (the life of the upper and middle classes) was to be romanticised forever as a golden age of lost innocence. Nor were class relations all that were fundamentally altered: states, too, learned how to 'intervene' and organise economic life. Everywhere, although war economies were quickly dismantled, the threshold of state economic power was higher, and the model of a war economy remained. Elements of this model were developed in the 'command economies' of the Soviet Union and Nazi Germany in the 1930s, while a more limited form of state intervention developed in 'New Deal' America under Roosevelt. (It was this triple experience of extending state power – rather than mere changes in ownership and control – which prompted James Burnham's famous 1940 critique of Marxism, *The Managerial Revolution*.[20]) Even where, as in Britain, the politics of non-intervention remained dominant, the state had learned many of the lessons of 1914–18 and was planning for war. The 'leisurely essay writing' of the Committee of Imperial Defence was replaced after 1935 with systematic planning for conscription, food control, a wartime restructuring of ministries, and building up war industries. Of course, 'believing that "industry ought not to be interfered with", the Government was attempting to impose rearmament upon recovery within an uncontrolled economy'.[21]

There is some historical debate about how far Germany had developed a war economy before 1939. The traditional view is that Germany had been on a war footing since 1935 or so: it has been pointed out that by 1938 Germany was devoting 25 per cent of its national income to military expenditure, Britain only 7 per cent.[22] Milward, however, argues that in Germany rearmament went in hand with economic recovery and that a great deal of state expenditure after 1933 – for example, the *Autobahn* programme – had a dual civil and military purpose. Nazi economics before 1939 was based on guns *and* butter: civilian consumption was not seriously reduced for some while even after war broke out. German war planning was based on the concept of *Blitzkrieg*, and hoped by this means to avoid being overwhelmed by the superior economic strength of its potential adversaries. It was also 'a method of avoiding the total economic commitment of "total war"'.[23] According to Milward, 'in September 1939 Germany had not yet ventured on the basic reorganisation of her economy which the war would eventually entail, whereas Britain had'.[24] Only the invasion of the Soviet Union finally exposed the weakness of the *Blitzkrieg* economy, creating severe strains which led from the winter of 1941–42 to more drastic reorganisation, restriction of consumer goods, etc. Yet, argues Milward, 'even in 1944 when German armaments production was so high, the economy could not be called a full war economy' – as a high production of consumer goods was maintained.[25]

Certainly, what this argument suggests is that there is no simple model of a 'war economy' which is switched over to at the outbreak of war. The nature of each war economy depends on the conception of war, economy and state which are dominant in the states themselves. These vary, not only according to the general character of the regime, but according to its specific policies (e.g. there were vast differences between the wartime economies of Germany itself, the occupied countries of Western Europe, and the enslaved areas to the East). They also vary according to the specific requirements of the war at different stages, although they may be far from expressing a 'rational' military-economic response (c.f. the Nazis' diversion of scarce resources to the extermination of Jews at the period of their greatest military weakness).

The Second World War was a total war in an even fuller sense than the First World War, therefore, not simply because its economic organisation was far more planned – although it was – but because of the unfolding demands of the conflict. In so many ways, however, the course of the Second World War was determined by the legacy of the First: not only because of state control and economic planning for war, but by the national-political ideologies which drove popular mobilisation, and in the military strategies and technologies involved. Indeed it was partly because of the way in which the military-technological threat to civilian populations reinforced national solidarities and ideologies that the war could not be stopped short at a *Blitzkrieg*, but developed into all-out struggle lasting for six years.

In the sense that the war was a war of mass armies, based on mass production of weapons, vehicles and supplies of all sorts, the Second World War continued the mode of warfare of the First. But politics and economics, strategy and technology combined to create a new phase of total war. States' controls over both economy and society were everywhere more thorough and complete, bearing strong resemblances to each other, but the ideologies of mobilisation reflected real differences in political systems. Fascism, Stalinist state socialism and Western democracy appeared as contrasting models of war mobilisation, offering different models of society after the war. Strategy and weaponry underwent similar changes on all sides, the innovations of 1914-18 becoming commonplace in 1939-45. Land warfare, avoiding the trenches, was dominated by the tank; aerial warfare was widely seen, both before and during the war, as crucial. Civilian populations as such, as well as the economic installations around which they lived, were now seen as legitimate targets. All the evidence, from Britain and Germany, that bombing reinforced rather than undermined civilian support for the war, instead of leading to its abandonment, only produced more blanket attacks on cities. Dresden, not an economic or military target, was destroyed in a firestorm in the closing months of the war in Europe. Hiroshima and Nagasaki testified to the war's greatest technical 'progress', when single atomic devices accomplished a scale of killing previously requiring thousands of bombs.

The interaction of military and political logic is evident. War required – as 1914-18 had already shown – the total mobilisation of the people. Political and ideological support was essential for economic and military achievement. Since this was true on both sides, the strategy of each had to be based on attacking the people as well as the army of the other. Such attacks in turn intensified the identification of the people with the state, its form of national ideology, and its political system. The Second World War not only seemed to be, but was, in a real sense, a war of political systems (although it was much else besides). This is what made it much harder for citizens to refuse their support for it than either the First World War (in which the politicisation of the conflict was far less complete) or, for reasons which will become apparent later, the preparations for the Third World War.

Nuclear war-economy

It has been argued above that total war is not a single mode of war, but a developing relationship between war and society. Within this relationship it is possible to distinguish various main strands – economic, political, strategic, technical – each of which develops according to its own logic, while affecting other sides of the process and contributing to the overall result. Each element can be seen as reinforcing the others in determining the overall direction of the movement towards the 'totalisation' of war.

War can be said to become 'total' in at least two main senses: on the one hand, in the sense most used by social scientists, that it more and more completely incorporates the whole of social life; and on the other, in the military (Clausewitzian) sense, that it increasingly becomes an 'absolute' struggle of life and death for states and peoples. In reality, these are but two sides of the same process. The political-economic totalisation of war both facilitates and requires the military-technological totalisation. This is why the atomic bomb on Hiroshima, which obliterated a city and threatened an era of war as total annihilation, represents a logical conclusion to a century of industrialised warfare.

If 1945 represents a crucial turning-point in processes which can be traced back to the 1840s, if not beyond, it presents us with a conclusion which is not yet final. In that sense, although an end-point to total war was now clear, a new phase of total war opened up. The end of the Second World War would, in any case, even without the emerging technological climax of atomic weaponry, have ushered in such a phase. After 1945 it was much more evident than after 1918 that the end of *a* war was not the end of war as a dominant social reality; or, to be more precise, not the end of the developing process of total war. The Third World War is widely held to have begun even before the Second World War ended. The rivalry of the United States and the Soviet Union was clear enough in the final stages of that war, and was one of the factors influencing the use of the atomic bomb on Japan. By the late 1940s this new conflict was clearly institutionalised and becoming known as the 'Cold War', to signify a deep opposition and the full potential for open war. By the early 1950s the Cold War had become 'hot' in the limited theatre of Korea, but stopped short of any escalation to global conflict. Whether the entire East–West conflict, which has been continuous since 1945, should be called the 'Cold War', or whether this term should be reserved for particularly frosty periods (late 1940s/early 1950s and, more problematically, the 1980s), is largely a semantic debate.[26] What is important is that the East–West conflict has been a crucial, defining reality for all economic, social and political change since 1945, and that it is necessary to see the entire period as a phase of total war. Only when this is clearly recognised does it become possible to discuss changes within the period.

It could clearly be seen, even in 1945, that the use of the atomic bomb marked not just the end of the Second World War but a turning point in war itself, but it took a decade or more for a real change in the mode of warfare to develop. Since at first only the US possessed atomic weapons, and in insufficient quantities for all-out war, the early period of East–West conflict was characterised by a continuation of the 1939-45 type of war-preparations while demobilising from wartime levels. So, although war economies were rapidly converted to the purposes of reconstruction, historically high levels of 'peacetime' military expenditure were maintained – and military demobilisation was soon halted by the Korean War. Mass armed forces based on conscription remained universal, although large resources were directed into research for an atomic arms race. Everywhere, too, in the period of reconstruction and the early Cold War, states retained the sort of economic supremacy which total war had given them. Only states – and to a large extent, only the USA, which alone was greatly strengthened by the war – could rebuild the many economies which were shattered. Both those states which emerged victorious and those which were rebuilt by the victors assumed central economic roles in national societies. The requirements of the new Cold War and of reconstruction combined to ensure this. The wartime experience of state economic direction, superimposed on the failure of private capitalism between the wars, gave credence to interventionist economics, reinforced by the political strength of the left in the immediate aftermath of the war.

The first decade after 1945 gave relatively little indication, therefore, of the fundamental change in the total war 'system' of war-society relationships in the nuclear age. The invention of atomic weapons was, however, a qualitative leap in the industrialisation of warfare. From now on, a very few weapons, which could be produced and operated by very few people, could decide the whole outcome of a major war. Such weapons have not, of course, replaced what are now known as 'conventional' weapons – these have continued to be required for secondary wars as well as to provide less destructive or supplementary fire power in a major war. Indeed the victory of technology involved much more than the development of the atomic bomb: constant technical innovation and refinement have become a major concern of military and political establishments at *all* levels of weaponry.

In an obvious sense the ultimate destructive potential of nuclear weapons had been created by the late 1950s or early 1960s. The superpowers had acquired 'overkill' – the capacity to totally destroy each other, and indeed human civilisation as a whole, recognised in the strategic doctrine of 'Mutually Assured Destruction'. But both despite and because of the strategic impasse which this represented, military-scientific innovation has continued to escalate well beyond this interim climax. The search has long been on for the technical 'fix' which will allow escape from the nuclear stalemate, whether in 'lower' levels of weaponry such as battlefield nuclear weapons or high-technology conventional armaments, or in the lofty, even fantastic realms of 'Star Wars'.

A great deal has been written about the links between the post-war arms race and the economy. On the one hand, it has been suggested that the alliance of the military and the industrial sectors dependent on them constitutes a military industrial complex, which dominates and directs American society in particular. C. Wright Mills's 1956 study of *The Power Elite* gave great weight to military-industrial linkages within a system of power which as a whole had increasingly been centralised by military conflict and nuclear technology.[27] Thompson argues, even more radically, that modern societies 'do not *have* military-industrial complexes – they *are* military-industrial complexes'.[28] For him, 'exterminism' is the driving force of the entire social system. On the other hand, more specifically economic analyses were put forward to suggest that Western (and, by implication, Eastern) systems were 'arms economies', in which arms production provided the central dynamic of the economic system as a whole. Originally developed during the Second World War and its immediate aftermath, especially Korea, as a theory of a Permanent War Economy, this was subsequently modified as it was recognised that nuclear weapons could inhibit major wars while stimulating military expenditure which had a fundamental economic effect. So the arms economy was presented as an explanation of the post-war boom.[29]

It is clear in retrospect that much of this analysis reflected a moment of transition in post-war militarism: the point at which the labour-intensive militarism of classical 'total war' was still strong, but the central significance of nuclear weapons was already clear. Theories of an arms economy, in particular, tended to amalgamate these two realities, seeing the nuclear arms race as the apex of an entire system of military expenditure. In one sense of course this was, and remains, true: even the most technologically advanced military force still comes down to soldiers with mass-produced weapons. But the trend has been to substitute machines – large-scale, highly complex and sophisticated machines – for men. Instead of soldiers with weapons, there are weapons-systems with their operators, as many of them concerned with maintenance as with actual use. (Today research is underway to replace soldiers with robots in some battlefield situations.) The warships which consumed such phenomenal sums in the naval arms race at the turn of the century were the precursors of modern armaments of all types, land and aerial as well as naval. The atomic bomb symbolises a new sort of militarism, scientifically and technologically based, and capital-intensive. While real spending on military purposes has soared, armies have become smaller and more professional. Although Britain remains an exception in having completely abandoned conscription, the relative importance of soldiers (especially conscripts) has generally declined.

The political economy of modern militarism necessarily differs from its mid-twentieth century predecessor. A large, immensely well-funded military sector in all major economies turns out equipment of a size, complexity and sophistication hardly matched in many civil industries. The gap is perhaps most notorious in the Soviet Union, which has sacrificed investment in civilian production to 'keep up' in the military field.[30] But, as Mary Kaldor has pointed out, American military technology – the world leader – is itself increasingly baroque: if not unusable (let us not repeat Engels's mistake), then difficult to use.[31] This is true both in a strategic sense, since technological refinement is increasingly cut off from viable military theory (a technical expression of the strategic impasse), and practically, since complex machines take a colossal effort to keep serviceable.

Military technology in the first half of the twentieth century required large workforces to produce its weapons, and large quantities of basic raw materials to make them with. Weapons and military vehicles were often similar in kind to non-military commodities (hence conversion from peace to war and war to peace was easier). Now, at the end of the twentieth century, military industries have become capital-intensive, use highly specialised materials and are often producing items of a kind which have little affinity with civilian production. Military industry may still affect the civilian economy, but often by producing distorted reflections of its own requirements rather than creating employment (as in earlier periods). The relationship between nuclear weapons production with its raw material, plutonium, and the civilian nuclear industry is a major case in point: the nuclear industry came into existence as a by-product of nuclear weapons and has been maintained by states for military and political as much as energy-policy reasons.[32] The nuclear industry is a sector of the civil economy which mirrors the military and the military-industrial sector in its high-technology, low-employment base, its skilled workforce and its security requirements.

A major paradox of the mid-century phase of total war was the association of warfare with welfare: even Nazi rearmament, we have noted, was based on guns *and* butter, and remained so until the war itself became a desperate struggle for the state's survival. The states which emerged from the Second World War all adopted historically advanced social policies, leading to rapidly expanding social expenditure simultaneous with high military spending. At the margin, the two forms of state activity competed for resources, but taking the early post-war period as a whole, both were vastly expanded compared to the inter-war years.[33] The post-war boom, however, was a triumph of private capitalism, emerging from its subordination in the war to take advantage of the post-war reconstruction. Military-industrial sectors played a leading economic role in the 1950s, but as the boom became self-sustaining, the proportion of military expenditure in most national incomes declined. Consumer goods industries were central to the boom, and the leading roles belonged to those countries which had relatively low military expenditures, notably Japan and West Germany. At the height of the boom, in the mid-1960s, and in the early stages of economic crisis, in the early 1970s, military expenditures were declining relative not only to national incomes, but also to state social expenditures.[34]

Only in the late 1970s, with the coincidence of deepening

economic crises and East–West tensions, did military expenditure begin to rise in relation to total production. This time, however, there was no apparently benign association of warfare and welfare: on the contrary, military expenditures were increased in a period of profound crisis for state spending as a whole, and grew at the expense of, rather than in conjunction with, various forms of social expenditure. Indeed, the paradox of the current phase is that military statism has been taken furthest by those Western governments that are most actively anti-statist in ideology. Instead of going in hand with welfare-statism, the new militarism is linked to high-technology, aggressive private-enterprise capitalism.

Social theory has been none too successful in unravelling such paradoxes. On the one hand, a major recent textbook by three Marxist writers, despite an informative account of the role of war, states and reconstruction in the origins of the post-war boom, treats the actual boom and its crisis in exclusively economic terms, making militarism once again a purely extraneous if not irrelevant factor.[35] On the other, Thompson offers his nightmare of a society which is, as a whole, 'exterminist': dominated by a military technology which is leading to its destruction. The polarisation of viewpoints reflects the difficulties of grappling with the present phase of the total war/society relationship. In the earlier phases, this relationship was manifestly central: militarism meant social mobilisation, and war carried this to an extreme. In the modern phase, militarism consumes massive resources but does *not* mobilise society.

Total war becomes less total in the sense of direct social participation at the very point at which it becomes greatly more total, indeed potentially absolute, in the military sense. Thus while in one sense it is utterly correct to see the entire global social system as conditioned by total war – in exterminist terms – much of social reality apparently contradicts this insight. The economic, social, even political and ideological links between the arms race and most social life become *less* direct, the more sophisticated and lethally accurate nuclear weaponry becomes. The nuclear arms race has largely been conducted out of sight of society, with states deliberately eschewing even ideological, let alone practical, mobilisation. Even in the United States, by far the most obviously militarist of Western societies, militarism and related political and nationalist ideologies are far less unequivocally dominant than they were in the 'Cold War' of the first decade after 1945. This has a great deal to do with the fact that the function of actual war has radically altered. War cannot be recognised unequivocally even as a possible outcome of war-preparation; and war, if it came, would not heighten social mobilisation as in all previous phases, but result in the most extreme demobilisation – physical destruction of the majority of society's members.

Here then we have an explanation for the paradox of modern militarism. As the strand of technological rivalry becomes dominant within the total war, society becomes simultaneously both more *and* less dominated by warfare. On the one hand, any major war would be so utterly decisive for society, that military preparations have an enormous priority over other social and political aims of states. They are not the only claimants on states' resources, and when military pressures recede, other interests are more effective: but in periods of active military–political tension, like the early 1980s, very impressive military–economic commitments are made. The Reagan administration could launch a military spending boom financed by budget deficits; the Soviet Union would attempt to match US military efforts, despite its weaker economy, thus continuing to spend roughly double the US proportion of its national income on 'defence'; even Britain under Thatcher could increase real military spending by 30 per cent between 1979 and 1985, in a period of economic stagnation and within a general policy of reducing state spending.[36]

On the other hand, all this can be accomplished without increasing the size of armies, extending or reintroducing conscription, or employing more people in defence industries.[37] Ideologically, the nuclear arms race, even with the excesses of Reagan's America, is muted compared to the jingoism of the pre-1914 period or the fervour of the early Cold War: it has more limited need of popular support. Of course, there is a major difference between the superpowers and the other industrialised states which are, for the most part, allied to them. Military preparations and the ideologies of militarism are both more important in the USA and the USSR than they are in Western or Eastern Europe or Japan. But even where militarism is stronger, its character has changed. The dominance of technology leads to a bifurcation between what Michael Mann has called the 'deterrence-science' militarism of the elite, and the 'spectator-sport' militarism of the mass.[38] If the majority of society continues to participate in militarism, it is in a passive, vicarious manner, since war-preparation requires only their tacit ideological consent, no longer their practical involvement. Short of all-out East–West war, most forms of militarism emanating from advanced industrial states – whether in the nuclear arms race or more actively in limited wars in the Third World (archetypally, in the Falklands/ Malvinas war, which will be discussed later) – require an extremely limited, controlled response from the majority of society. This circumstance utterly transforms the politics of total war, and should lead us to question the main forms of response to war which emerged earlier in this century and are still dominant today.

The Politics of Total War I:
Revolution, Totalitarianism and War

If the political economy of militarism has changed with each major phase of total war, so too has its politics and sociology. Indeed, we can say that each phase of total war has had its characteristic political forms, corresponding both to the demands which war-preparation makes on society and the contradictions of that process. The rest of this book will discuss three major forms of radical politics associated with the development of total war: the particular models of revolution and social reform associated with the first and second periods of total war, and what I shall at this point call the 'radical politics of the nuclear age'.

It must be emphasised that while broad links are made between forms of politics and phases of total war, no absolute, one-to-one links are being proposed. Each period contains more than one form of politics and each form of politics – which may have its own contradictions – spans more than one period. Similarly, I should not wish to suggest that total war provides the only context in which political developments can be understood. Historians and theorists have long tried to understand political change in other, more familiar, economic and social contexts. The argument here does not aim to cancel all existing interpretations, but rather to systematically discuss the relationship of politics to war-making – a relationship which, where it has been discussed at all, has tended to be discussed incidentally (since war is not 'normal'). The argument, essentially, is that the development of total war has decisively shaped the process of political change. The analytical framework of phases of total war, corresponding to particular political forms, is a means of structuring the discussion and enabling us to follow through historical changes in a way which focusses on the relationships.

Revolutionary origins of total war

We have already noted that France in the Revolutionary and Napoleonic period offers a primitive model of the national economic and political mobilisation characteristic of total war. War mobilisation of the French people was as complete as the technology, communications and bureaucracy of the time could make it. And war, as Skocpol argues, 'was far from extrinsic to the development and fate of the French Revolution; rather it was central and constitutive, just as we would expect from knowing the nature and dilemmas of the Old Regime from which the Revolution sprang'.[1] Her case is that the Revolution reflected not simply the social and economic contradictions affecting the classes in French society – stressed by many historians – but the crisis of the old state. The *ancien régime* was unable to develop the finance, administration and military power necessary to realise its military ambitions.[2]

The Revolution cleared the way for a much larger, more centralised, state apparatus, able to exploit its revolutionary-patriotic ideology and new means of coercion to mobilise large armies and the economic resources for major wars. The Revolution inevitably upset the balance of the European states system, in which France was centrally situated; and it created plenty of reasons on both sides for the series of wars which quickly unfolded. War, in turn, drastically affected the course of the Revolution, delivering the '*coup de grace* to the liberal phase of 1789-91',[3] and creating both the bureaucracy of *La France fonctionnaire*[4] and the elements of a professional officer corps and a modern national army. Not for the last time, therefore, a social revolution was instrumental in bringing about a major development of the state machine (Marx, incidentally, recognised this in the French case: where he erred was in believing that proletarian revolution would have a different result).

Whatever the contribution of wars to the crisis of the old order, warfare had not directly produced the Revolution in France. The Revolution was *sui generis* (or, at least, the product of political and social crisis): revolution led to war, not the other way round. And the French war effort owed its decisive characteristics – popular nationalism, mass participation, as well as centralised coercion and administration – to the Revolution. The Revolution made a reality of the concept of citizenship; included in this concept were not only the rights of citizens but their duties towards the nation, of which the highest was that of military service – to die, if need be, for France.

Such ideals were capable of serving the interests of many forms of state, not just a democratic republic. In France, of course, revolutionary warfare led to military dictatorship and ultimately to the Empire of Napoleon. Elsewhere in Europe, during the nineteenth century, as states of all kinds adapted to the changes in warfare brought about by the Revolutionary and Napoleonic period and later by industrialisation, they utilised such revolutionary contributions for their own ends. Conscription became normal for continental states; mass armies on a new scale came into existence. Alongside the extension of military service was the adoption of forms of constitutional government which recognised, albeit to greatly varying degrees, the rights of conscriptable citizens. In addition, recognising the danger that even limited democracy could be utilised by socialist or revolutionary movements which might not accept the regimes' goals, states fostered popular nationalism for their own ends. By the end of the century – with the assistance of right-wing parties, an emerging mass-circulation press, religious and other supports – the nationalism which in France had served Revolution and Republic could now work equally well for King, Kaiser, or even Tsar. In this sense, the revolutionary model of warfare was the normal one, in the age of emerging total war.

Contradictions of mass militarism

It was correctly foreseen by Friedrich Engels that, as mass militarism was cut off from its revolutionary origins, it nonetheless generated new revolutionary possibilities within itself.

> The army has become the main purpose of the state, and an end in itself; the peoples are only there in addition in order to provide and feed the soldiers. Militarism dominates and is swallowing Europe. But this militarism also carries in itself the seeds of its own destruction.

Here is a direct analogy, by one of the founders of Marxism, between militarism and capitalism (which, of course, according to Marx's theory, will also be overthrown as a result of its internal contradictions). Engels points to a revolutionary dialectic in the mode of warfare itself:

> Competition of the individual states with each other forces them, on the one hand, to spend more money each year on the army and navy, artillery, etc. – thus more and more hastening financial catastrophe; and on the other hand, to take universal compulsory military service more and more seriously, thus in the long run making the whole people familiar with the use of arms; and therefore making the whole people able at a given moment to make its will prevail in opposition to the commanding military lords. And this moment comes as soon as the mass of the people – town and country workers and peasants – has a will. At this point the armies of princes become transformed into armies of the people; the machine refuses to work, and militarism collapses by the dialectic of its own evolution.[5]

This passage has been quoted at length because it beautifully expresses *one side* of the dialectic of war – 'the bursting asunder of militarism *from within*', as Engels goes on to describe it[6] – in the first phase of total war. What is wrong with it, as a finished position on the dialectics of total war and society, is that at best it describes only one side of a double-edged process. Furthermore (although this is no criticism of Engels, who could not have been expected to have prophesied developments in the mid and late-twentieth centuries), the process as a whole belongs, at least in the form in which Engels presents it, to a particular phase in the development of total war which is long past.

The partial validity of Engels's analysis is that the break-down of national armies in wars did indeed provide by far the most favourable conditions for social revolution in late nine-teenth- and early twentieth-century Europe. Wars were the prime contexts of revolutions, from the Paris Commune of 1871 to the Russian Revolution of 1905 and, above all, the 1917 Revolution and the upheavals which followed in Germany and Hungary at the end of the First World War. Wars were uniquely capable of causing states to disintegrate; of turning the working class and, in Russia, the peasantry into revolu-tionary forces; and of turning soldiers, as Engels foresaw, into armed revolutionaries.

The correctness of Engels's analysis only underlines the analytical problem for mainstream Marxism. Engels's argu-ment gives full weight, *ad hoc*, to the contradictions of what Kaldor calls the mode of warfare, something which on a general theoretical level he did not recognise at all (nor indeed did Marx). Unless we are to suggest that mass militarism can be directly reduced to the labour-intensive economy of nine-teenth-century capitalism – merely as an epiphenomenon – then there is a major analytical issue lurking here. This issue is also touched on in the classic turn-of-the-century Marxist text, Karl Liebknecht's *Militarism and Anti-Militarism*. After arguing, quite predictably, that each form of class society calls forth its own militarism, so that the contemporary form is 'capitalist militarism' – characterised by an army based on universal military service – Liebknecht acknowledges the overriding power of militarism.

> It is the final regulator, now secret, now open, of all class politics, of the tactics in the class struggle not only of the capitalist classes, but also of the proletariat, as much in its trade union organisation as in its political organisation.[7]

This formula certainly presents militarism as determining, rather than simply being determined by, social development.

The one-sidedness of Engels's argument is, moreover, an indication that these insights were far from fully absorbed into his thinking. It is not that Engels was unaware of the military consequences of revolution: he wrote enthusiastically of the changes in warfare which the armed people had brought about. What he failed to emphasise was the danger to the social and political goals of revolution, arising from their necessary military consequences. The Napoleonic outcome of the French Revolution represented, to Marx and Engels, no general problem of militarism-in-revolutions, but an expression of the bourgeois, state-centralising character of the French experience.

Engels's failure to see any general problem also reflected his enthusiasm for military strategy. He analysed changes in weapons and armies; he absorbed military ideas, such as those of Clausewitz; he effectively founded a tradition of Marxist military science which has appealed to 'Marxist' states and armies ever since.[8] He analysed the contradictions of 'capitalist' militarism, not as an opponent of militarism in general, but as a revolutionary for whom political strategy included an important military dimension. Although his thought anticipates the anti-militarism of the German revolutionaries, Liebknecht and Luxemburg, it also foreshadows the Clausewitzian Marxism of the Soviet armed forces.

That Engels was right to see the mass militarism of total war as a source of revolutionary contradictions in its own right, but fatally mistaken in not learning from France the consequences of militarism for the revolution, is demonstrated by the classic case of the Russian Revolution. Here we see the dialectics of the first phase of total war in their clearest, and most destructive expression.

War as the arbiter of revolution[9]

The mode of warfare is crucial to the Russian Revolution in two ways. On the one hand, without the climax of mass militarism in the First World War, there would have been no revolution; on the other, without the civil war, the outcome of the revolution would almost certainly have been very different. (Equally, the Russian Revolution played a key role in the transition in the mode of warfare from the first to the second phase of total war, as we shall discuss later).

The point behind these assertions is not to engage in counter-factual history, but to indicate the decisive role of war in the actual process of the Russian Revolution. Certainly, fundamental weaknesses in the state system and economy of Tsarist Russia, and antagonisms between classes, explain why Russia – rather than any other society, say the United States, Britain, or France – should have been plunged by the war into a social revolution. But it was war which in 1917, as in 1905, exposed these weaknesses, and aroused these antagonisms to the pitch of revolt. In particular, the disintegration of the Tsarist army under the pressure of the war realised Engels's prophetic remarks, quoted above: militarism did indeed 'burst asunder from within'. Crucial sections of the army turned their guns on their officers and became armed units of the Revolution. And soldiers were not only an essential part of revolutionary power; they were also a crucial social cement between the urban proletariat and the peasantry, without which the initial revolutionary synthesis would not have been possible.

Just as military failures, both in battle and in the supply of armies, were not unique to Russia, so were revolutionary soldiers a more widespread phenomenon. The German defeat led, at the end of 1918, to mutinies and to the setting up of soldiers' and sailors' councils, which with similar councils among the workers were the backbone of the German Revolution. And of course it was not just soldiers who were revolutionised by the war: total war meant a massive mobilisation of the entire working class, eliminating unemployment, recruiting women into the workforce, and making drastic changes in workers' conditions and political situation. While war-mobilisation initially had the effect of suppressing class conflict, in the longer run it stimulated it, even in the more stable and victorious states such as Britain and the USA. Workers' confidence was increased by full employment; organisation grew; militancy was provoked by arbitrary war measures; and as the popular patriotism of mobilisation gave way to disillusionment, radical and revolutionary ideologies spread. Only in Russia did a revolutionary movement achieve and retain power; but 1918-19 was the highpoint of a revolutionary wave in Central Europe, and possibly the closest even Britain has been (although not very close) to a revolutionary situation in modern times.[10]

The mass movements at the end of the war expressed a widespread weariness with, rather than popular opposition to, the war – in the countries of the victorious Allies as well as the defeated powers. The most radical movements were led, however, by socialists who had stood out against the war and formed the internationalist opposition within European socialism. Indeed the revolutionary leaders now thrust to the fore had formed the left wing even inside the anti-war Zimmerwald movement (named after the conference of anti-war socialists in 1915). The revolutionary events at the war's close were a vindication of the anti-militarist Marxism of leaders such as Liebknecht and Luxemburg in Germany, and Lenin and Trotsky in Russia. Their triumph was short-lived, however, since the German Revolution was soon crushed, its leaders murdered; and the Russian Revolution, like the French more than a century before, soon posed problems of militarism which were hardly foreseen by its leaders.

There was, in any case, a difference of emphasis, especially between Luxemburg and Lenin, which reflected the contradictions in which Marxists found themselves over modern militarism. Luxemburg was far more impressed with the sheer horrors of the First World War, and her speeches and writings are imbued with a passionate anti-militarism. Certainly, she saw the war as creating the conditions for revolution, advocated the arming of the people, and wrote that

> The struggle for socialism is the mightiest civil war that history has ever seen, and the proletarian revolution must prepare the necessary tools for this civil war, and must learn to use them – to fight and win.[11]

But she also expressed a profound abhorrence of bloodshed. There is much to suggest that she was using the term 'civil war' as little more than alternative formulation for 'class struggle'. Although she undoubtedly recognised the military dimension to the revolution, she seems to have mentally subordinated this – as did most Marxists before the actual experience of civil war – to the political and economic aspects of class struggle (rather as international relations writers talk of 'conflict' between states, as if this makes it more manageable than 'war').

Lenin, on the other hand, while formally as opposed to (capitalist) militarism as Luxemburg, hinged his wartime strategy on the concept of 'revolutionary defeatism'. He argued that revolutionaries should work everywhere for the defeat of their 'own' imperialists, and to turn imperialist into civil war. While Lenin had no clearer intimation than Luxemburg of the character of the eventual civil war in Russia – this eluded all the revolutionaries – the thrust of his arguments was different. Where Luxemburg worked for resistance to the war, and for socialism as a means to end its horrors, Lenin aimed more single-mindedly at power, including the need to take up arms to achieve it.

In order to win power, the propaganda of the Russian

Bolsheviks had worked with the popular mood of war-weariness among the workers, peasants – and soldiers. The problem of militarism in the Russian Revolution arose in part, ironically, from its very completeness as a revolution against militarism. The peasants-in-uniform who had rebelled within the Tsar's army had no wish to remain in a democratic, revolutionary army to defend the soviets against counterrevolution. Their desire for peace was total, and there was little the Bolsheviks could do after October to prevent the revolutionary units disintegrating, and the peasants returning to the land. When civil war came, the remnants of the army and workers' militia were manifestly insufficient to fight off a battery of forces. The logic of the situation demanded a massive new effort to organise an armed force, or Soviet power and the Bolshevik regime might well have fallen.

The Red Army was therefore founded as a standing army, highly centralised, disciplined, and employing a large part of the old officer corps. Although its founder, Trotsky, in theory favoured the kind of militia-based army advocated by the French socialist Jean Jaurès, this was not seen as workable under the desperate conditions faced by the new Soviet regime. Indeed, as Deutscher explains, 'When he set out to found the Red Army, Trotsky seemed to be burning all that he had worshipped and worshipping all that he had burned.'[12] Militarism and discipline, centralisation and command, all of which the Bolsheviks had denounced, were now the order of the day.

The remilitarisation of the Revolution was not incidental to its progress. Just as the French Revolution moved quickly into military expansion, so the Russian Revolution, once the Red Army started to defeat its enemies within Russia's own borders, began their fateful 'export of revolution'. By 1920 Soviet forces, having defeated Pilsudski's Poles in Russia itself, were chasing them to Warsaw, thus breaching, as Deutscher again points out, the fundamental Marxist canon 'that revolution cannot and must not be carried on the point of bayonets into foreign countries' (a canon which was 'based on the experience of the French Revolution which found its fulfilment and also its undoing in Napoleonic conquest').[13]

Revolution, which in the Russian case – typically of twentieth-century revolutions – was born of war, gave rise to further war. Revolution is a social process which, because it involves the overthrow of an existing state form, always involves the possibility – indeed likelihood – of armed conflict between the old state and the new. Revolution is therefore always likely to include a process of military struggle, an element of civil war. It is possible to believe that taken in isolation, as the events in Petrograd in October 1917 show, a revolution may have sufficiently deep and wide popular support to render the military process secondary, or even minor. What is less probable is that revolution is possible without provoking some armed response from elements of the old state, the wider ruling class, or other states – the latter either because they see their interests threatened by revolution, or because they see an unstable new regime as offering scope for their own expansion (in the case of Russia, both). What this means is that while revolution and civil war may be chronologically distinct moments, they are necessarily linked as parts of the same process. A revolution which does not immediately, directly, become a civil war, is nevertheless likely to lead to civil war as the forces of counter-revolution form.

The problem of war, especially civil war, for a social revolution is that it inevitably generates the strong state-centralising pressures which were long ago seen in France. Only well-rooted social institutions, with extremely strong popular involvement, are likely to withstand the pressures of war. The demands of war, in any form of state, tend to override other social forces: the demands of revolutionary war, and above all civil war, in which the intensity of the leaders' commitment may be even greater, are likely to be stronger still. Social forms will continue to exist only to the extent that they are seen as necessary for the revolutionary state's survival in its struggle.

This problem was discussed, ironically, by Marxists writing

about capitalist states during the 1914-18 war. Lenin, Bukharin, Luxemburg and Liebknecht all saw the demands of war eclipsing the freedoms of civil society, and undermining bourgeois parliamentary democracy. Lenin, for example, saw the war as making the advanced countries into 'military conflict prisons for the workers'; Luxemburg believed that only socialism could offer hope of any form of democracy after the war.[14] These were not implausible views at the time, since the war was accompanied by sharp repression of socialists, trade unionists and pacifists in the most democratic of the belligerent states. It also undermined the basis for stable parliamentary democracy in much of Central and Southern Europe, as the years after 1918 were to show. And yet in most of the core countries of Western capitalism, especially in North-Western Europe and North America, 'democracy' was to survive and to remain capitalism's dominant political form.

The irony is that if any state immediately and graphically demonstrated the thesis that war reduces democracy, it was Soviet Russia itself. Here, soviet institutions (the councils of workers', soldiers' and peasants' deputies), the democratic basis of the revolution, were quickly undermined by civil war. In part this was because, in contrast to the successful war efforts of, say, the USA or Britain, the Bolsheviks' civil war reverses *demobilised* their urban economy and dispersed the revolutionary working class. But soviet institutions were undermined equally because their vitality was not a priority compared to the pressing military demands, and indeed was seen as an obstacle to victory. The abandonment of the democratic principle in the army became a model for society: the military principle of command was universally applied. The 'barracks society', Liebknecht's original Marxist nightmare of capitalist militarism, was actually realised in Soviet Russia, in a system which became known as 'war communism'. The Bolshevik leaders' enthusiasm for this desperate expedient – Trotsky's desire to militarise workers in labour battalions, Bukharin's belief that war was class struggle raised to a higher plane – was the most grotesque aspect of the period. Here, rather than in the revolutionary ideology *per se* – and to add to the irony, among Stalin's future opponents – lie the intellectual as well as the practical antecedents of Stalin's totalitarianism.

Stalinist totalitarianism and total war

The civil war did not of course bring Stalin into power; it accomplished the transition from the revolutionary soviet-based state of 1917 to the party-state of the 1920s. Further attrition within the party, and the 'revolution from above' launched at the end of the decade, would be necessary to transform that state into Stalin's terroristic, totalitarian monolith.[15] Undoubtedly, the deepest influences on this transformation of Soviet Russia were those of power itself, its consolidation and exercise. But it was power exercised in a context: not just in a Russian society with continuing industrial backwardness and a mass-peasant base, but in an unstable European and global state-system. Given the failure of the Tsarist war-machine in 1914-17 and the incursions of the civil war, Russia's new rulers feared above all that they might be exposed to a threat from the West. The root of the crash industrialisation programme and the subordination of agriculture was the need to create an industrial base to support a military machine, strong enough to withstand German militarism. After 1933, with Hitler in power, the threat was increasingly obvious rather than hypothetical.

The totalitarianism of Stalin's Russia was, then, rooted in total war. War had provoked the Revolution; the civil war had shaped the party-state; the drive to military power was a major force in Stalin's 'second revolution'. The Stalinist state created an economic system strikingly reminiscent of the wartime economies of 1914-18: a command economy in which all was subordinate to the requirements of the central state. There was a difference, however, between such a command economy and a war economy. In the Soviet Union before 1939 (or, indeed, 1941), although military production had a high priority and the construction of basic heavy industry was effectively the construction of a military infrastructure, the system was not geared completely to the single purpose of all-out war. And yet all-out war was the real test of the Soviet state and economy. In the 'Great Patriotic War', precisely because of the appalling suffering and death toll of the Soviet people, society was bonded with the state. War-mobilisation and ultimate victory legitimised the Stalinist system. They remain to this day a key reference point of the state's ideology, surviving Stalin himself and the transformation of his system of terror into a more 'normal' mode of bureaucratic repression.

Stalinism has often been seen by its Marxist critics as a form of internal counter-revolution. It replaced the popular, revo-lutionary-democratic rule of workers' and peasants' soviets with a vicious dictatorship over the working class, and elimi-nated genuine revolutionary traditions, leaders and collective party organisation in favour of monolithic personal rule. The 'revolution from above' was actually a brutal, violent counter-revolution by the Stalinist party-state against the basic classes of Russian society. It was accomplished by means of liqui-dating the peasantry, imposing a draconian regime in the factories, and terrorising peasants, workers and bureaucrats alike with an immense system of labour camps.

If the Russian Revolution of 1917 can be seen as reflecting the inner contradictions in a total war society, the Stalin regime was that society in permanent, ongoing form. The discipline, degradation and death of the camps directly echoed that of the trenches in 1914-18: with the difference that while the danger of bombardment was removed, so was the promise of release. The labour discipline of Soviet heavy industry far surpassed that of the munitions factories of the Great War. The ideology of party, leader and 'ism' also went far beyond, while indeed it incorporated, the simpler patriot-ism of earlier times. Here we can begin to see the importance of Stalinism, not just as a reflection of a total war society, but also as a development of it. Moreover, a society which was held together by armed force, accustomed to the systematic arbitrariness of state terror, was also one which was prepared – insofar as it is ever possible to be prepared – for the horror of the 'higher' phase of total war. For in 1939-45, war was to physically envelop civilian populations on a scale which dwarfed that of 1914-18, and nowhere more so than in the Soviet Union. While the purges of the 1930s certainly had some negative military consequences, there is also a sense in which Stalin's terror prepared Soviet society for the worst.

Nazism: total war and genocide

This connection between totalitarianism and total war is at its clearest in Nazism. While the manifest ideological roots of Stalinism lay in the rational, scientific tradition of European socialism, Nazism's much looser antecedents were in the murkier reactions to the claims of science and reason. While Stalinism might be said, despite all its barbarity, to have completed the industrialisation of Russia, no such historic task can be attributed to Nazism. And while the origins of Stalin's counter-revolutionary terror have to be traced through several contradictory phases – from the initial revolutionary disintegration of militarism, through its civil war recomposition to its eventual Stalinist incarnation – there are no such complexities in the Nazi process. The stages in Nazism are those of a tradition which was, from its origins, both counter-revolutionary and militarist to the core. While in one sense, this contrast makes Stalinism appear worse – the triumph of totalitarian, counter-revolutionary militarism over rational-socialist, revolutionary-democratic, anti-militarist origins – Nazism presents itself as the political nadir of the era of total war.

Whatever antecedents can be sought for fascism, either in general or in its specifically Nazi form, the phenomenon itself clearly emerged from the First World War. The experience of Italy's national humiliation turned Mussolini, originally a socialist, towards what became fascism. Germany's ultimate defeat and the losses imposed upon it at Versailles were crucial to the formation of Hitler's National Socialists. The war gave them their aims – to restore wounded nationalisms to a new form of glory; their methods – militaristic political movements which borrowed many forms from the mass armies; and many of their initial recruits – the rejected, often unemployed, former soldiers for whom defeat meant the loss of vocation. Nazism, in particular, emerged from a plethora of reactionary, militarist movements (such as the notorious Freikorps who murdered Luxemburg and Liebknecht) which developed in the fluid aftermath of the war.

Socialist accounts of fascism have generally stressed what was unique about it, compared to other forms of reactionary or right-wing politics: that it was a mass counter-revolutionary movement based largely on the middle class and the unemployed working class. They have seen it as a response both to capitalist crisis and to the revolutionary movements of the working class seeking to resolve that crisis in a socialist direction. Fascist repression and militarism represented an alternative solution to the crisis, still within the bounds of capitalism. Of the major Marxist writers, only Paul Sweezy clearly specifies however that fascism is a product of 'war-damaged capitalism', arguing that 'a prolonged and "unsuccessful" war is the only social phenomenon sufficiently catastrophic to set in train this particular chain of events.'[16] And yet subsequent events support this judgement, made in 1942; the economic crises of Western capitalism in the 1970s and 1980s have been sufficient to give some new impetus to fascist movements, but nowhere anything like enough to make them major political forces seriously contending for power.

Fascist parties, growing in those capitalist societies most 'injured' by the First World War, were militaristic mass movements seeking to restore their nations' power. Militarism was a major part of their ideology, and fascist states enhanced the position of the armed forces as well as creating specifically fascist military forces (e.g. the Waffen SS). The centrality of militarism to fascism explains the affinity between fascist movements, strictly defined, and cases such as Franco's Spain (a military counter-revolution leading to the personal dictatorship of a military leader, borrowing from the politics and economics of fascism), and Imperial Japan (a militarily expansionist dictatorship). The propensity to use their military forces in expansionist ventures varied greatly, of course, in proportion to the strength and geopolitical position of the states: Spain, after its civil war, actually remained neutral in the Second World War; Italy's independent ventures were limited to the Abyssinian expedition and other relatively minor interventions (including Spain), until it was drawn into Hitler's war; while Germany and Japan were, of course, the driving forces of the European and Pacific wars.

In the prototypical case of Nazism, as in that of its non-identical twin, Stalinism, the use of massive violence for political and ideological ends – which had accompanied the rise of each to power – flourished in conditions of full total war. In Stalin's war, the system of labour camps, already huge in the 1930s, reached its awful peak; whole nationalities were transported from one end of the Soviet Union to another. In Hitler's war, the concentration camps swelled with the conquered peoples, above all the Jews. The fateful steps to mass extermination, however much they were anticipated by persecution from the earliest days of the Reich, could only occur under the cover of total war. As millions died and millions more were moved across continents, all under conditions of military secrecy and complete press censorship, it was uniquely possible for the Nazis to systematically organise the worst horrors which had been abstractly indicated in their racist doctrines. Only the war, indeed, placed in Hitler's hands the huge populations of Jews and other racial undesirables who were outside the borders of the pre-war Reich.

In this sense, Nazism represents the politics most finely tuned to the realities of total war. Nazism utterly embraced the murderous technical logic which turned millions of civilians into legitimate military targets. It made a virtue of what others still called necessity. The mass killing of soldiers in the trenches had, by 1939-45, become the mass killing of civilians in aerial bombardments: each was justified, albeit dubiously, with military argument. The killing of the camps had no such rationale imposed on it: and yet it was part of the Nazi war effort because the war, for Hitler, was a campaign of mass slaughter against Jews and other racial enemies as well as a conventional military campaign against enemy states. As Calleo has recently suggested:

> To observe that race policy was fatally impolitic or seriously interfered with the conduct of the war is to miss the point. Racial policy was the object of the war.[17]

At this point, the links between totalitarianism and total war become clearer. Totalitarianism is a political tendency which expresses two related developments in total war: the militarisation of politics and the politicisation of war. We cannot be certain whether to judge Hitler's extermination of the Jews in military or ideological terms, because it is not clear where ideology ends and strategy begins. This is an extreme expression of general processes, certainly, but they are there. In 1939-45, on all sides, there were political goals as well as state interests, competing political systems as well as territorial aims.

Politics in the second phase of total war

We have finally come to what was meant by suggesting that the Russian Revolution played a key role in the transition between the first and the second phases of total war. In the First World War, ideology – in relatively simple forms of nationalism and patriotism, roughly comparable in the various combatant states – was a means by which states mobilised their populations. Although political goals were incorporated into the way in which nationalism was presented – for example, the Anglo-American emphasis on democracy fighting against unbridled Prussian militarism – this was a subordinate element. What is more, it failed to convince significant minorities, both in the intellectual middle class and in working-class movements, who maintained some sort of opposition to the war.

The Russian Revolution, erupting from the contradictions of this first phase of total war, began a process of the politicisation of warfare which was fully realised in 1939-45. As early as the civil war, Bolshevik leaders (notably Bukharin in his left phase) produced the theory that class war was being replaced by war between capitalist and proletarian states as the central revolutionary process.[18] This was of course a deviation from orthodox Marxism, since it substituted the Soviet state for the revolutionary proletariat of the capitalist countries as the main agency of change. But, as we have seen, it corresponded to the practice of the Red Army's attempts to export the revolution, and it anticipated the new Stalinist orthodoxy which subordinated the international revolution to the interests of the Soviet state – in peace or war, depending on its changing requirements. The Stalinist state justified every twist and turn of its policy in terms of the ideology of international Communism, and was in turn presented in this light by its enemies in the West.

The victory of Nazism rapidly advanced the politicisation of international conflict as well as the likelihood of a second world war. Nazism had long identified Bolshevism and international capitalism as Jewish evils on a world scale, and Germany's new imperialism was inseparable from the struggle against them. This left international conflict polarised, for the first time, between major states with sharply contrasting political systems and ideologies: Soviet Communism, German National Socialism and the Western democracies. The two totalitarian states pursued an economic and political mobilisation of their population which was reminiscent of the general war-mobilisation of 1914-18, but with new ideological fervour. Only the democracies – while not neglecting war-planning – eschewed social mobilisation. The consequences of the new phase of international conflict could be seen in Spain in 1936-39, when the civil war became for the fascist powers and, to a lesser extent, the Soviet Union, an international, ideological war. Only Britain and France refused to see the war in such terms, and withheld any significant support from the Spanish Republic, which was after all a parliamentary democracy.

The politicisation of total war in its second phase was therefore well advanced by the outbreak of the Second World War: only in the democracies was war itself necessary to turn the political system into a specific form of war-mobilisation. The consequences, in Britain after 1940, and rather less markedly in the White Dominions and later in the USA, were significant modifications in the political system. While the state became more centralised – as had the totalitarian states, and as indeed Marxist critics had seen as an inevitable consequence of total war way back in 1914-18 – it depended more on the implicit support of society. A tacit contract was developed, in which the state promised and even partially began social reform, in return for the people's commitment to the war effort. The contest with fascism sharpened the meaning of 'democracy' as a political system and ideology, as will be discussed in the next chapter.

Stalinism, Western democracy and fascism can therefore be seen as competing models of war-mobilisation – technically similar in important respects (e.g. in their use of propaganda) because of fighting the same war at a similar stage of military-technological development, but substantively quite different. The differences of system, between the two totalitarian models and even more between Western democracy and its fascist enemies, were seen as extremely significant by the majority of society. The social groups who in some Western countries had sustained opposition to the First World War provided consistent support for the war effort in 1939-45. (Equally, those who oppose preparations for a third, nuclear, world war are likely to look back on the Second as a justifiable conflict.[19])

The political conflict between the democracies and fascism became, therefore, the basic meaning of the war for many people in Western countries. And, in good part, this *is* what it was about: the Allied victory led to the consolidation of parliamentary democracies (with significant social reform) in most Western industrial states.[20] It was not all that the war was about, of course: this political conflict was interwoven with the more basic conflict of individual states, between and within alliances of states, involving their economic and strategic interests. But whereas, in 1914-18, such interests had been the main motives for the war, and national ideologies little more than supports for states, now the ideologies (reflecting different political systems) mattered as a direct and material part of the aims of the war. This was, moreover, a unique phase in the history of total war; for although competition of ideologies and political systems continued to dominate warfare after 1945, nuclear weapons rapidly make it impossible to envisage a war between the major powers which could meaningfully be seen as a fight over such principles.

Revolutionary warfare: its historical limits

The politicisation of warfare grew, it has been suggested, out of the militarisation of revolution. Another manifestation of this inner transformation of total war was the rise in the 1930s, and reaching a peak during the Second World War, of new forms of revolutionary warfare. Civil war was no longer a particular phase of a revolutionary process, an outcome of revolution itself: war and politics were now fused in a constant process of revolutionary civil war.

Guerilla warfare was not new, of course: it could be traced back to the Revolutionary and Napoleonic era, and in one sense was an inevitable outcome of the involvement of the people in war. (In the Peninsular War, *against* the export of the Revolution.) Once the people fight for what they see as their own purposes, once revolutionary or patriotic spirit becomes as important a component of war as the military hierarchy, irregular and unorthodox methods become more viable. Guerilla struggle is in a sense a prototype of modern total war, since the guerilla requires, often in a very direct and immediate way, the support of the people which states have to mobilise through a battery of centralised means.

Guerilla warfare was not, however, a part of classical revolutionary strategy; nor did it play any major role in the revolutions of the first quarter of the twentieth century. In Russia, as we have seen, the civil war succeeded the revolution, and even in the civil war, guerilla action was not dominant. It was the failure of the Communist uprising in the cities of China in 1925, and their subsequent persecution by their erstwhile allies of the Kuomintang, which forced a major revolutionary party to develop a new strategy. By the end of the decade the Chinese Communists under Mao Zedong were beginning their long struggle to win military control of China, starting in the more remote rural areas and only capturing the cities after 20 years of war.

China was a large country, with poor communications, uniquely fragmented between a weak central government, local warlords and foreign powers. Only in these circumstances could an initially small revolutionary force gradually build up its strength and extend its area of control. From the beginning the Communist struggle was a military one, but it built on political support from the peasantry in the areas it controlled. The Revolution has been reasonably described as a 'synthesis between the military needs of the Chinese Communists and the social-revolutionary potential of the Chinese peasantry'.[21] The Communists needed the peasants' support to sustain their armies with recruits and supplies; in return they encouraged and provided a military-administrative framework for social change. The Chinese Communist Party was never a peasant party in the sense in which the Russian Bolsheviks were a workers' party; nor did it possess the same sort of internal diversity and democracy. As a force engaged primarily in a military struggle, it was clearly controlled by its leaders, and peasant 'participation' was limited to the local level.

What gave the Chinese Revolution its greatest impetus was the war against the Japanese invaders from 1937, which eventually became part of the Second World War. The Japanese were more able to occupy the cities, where the Kuomintang were based, than the rural areas, where Communist guerillas were strong. This enabled the Communists to change the balance of forces with the Kuomintang and eventually to defeat them, in the renewed civil war after the defeat of Japan.[22]

The circumstances of foreign invasion in world war were a widespread condition for guerilla struggle in 1939-45. Occupation removed national and colonial regimes which, whatever questionable features they possessed, usually had some legitimacy. In their place were regimes based directly on force. Even if the occupiers (especially the Japanese) made attempts to summon up support for puppet or collaborationist rulers by exploiting national sentiment against colonial rule, they were hardly able to secure universal acceptance of their right to govern. A large part of the population in many countries would give at least tacit support to armed struggle against occupation, in the name of national liberation. Guerilla action was by no means the exclusive preserve of Communists, but they proved the most successful practitioners, actually seizing power in Yugoslavia and Albania, laying the foundations for an extraordinarily long but ultimately successful revolution in Vietnam, and laying claim to a major post-war political role by their work in the Italian and French resistance movements.

In historical perspective, the 1940s were the peak of the major, most successful period of guerilla struggle as a means of political change. This was the result of the coincidence of widespread occupation with the deeper contradictions of total war in its politicised phase. Mobilisation under universalistic political doctrines aroused movements for national independence in the colonies of the European democracies. Where the European empires retained physical control, as the British did in India, the national movements increased their pressure. A combination of repression and concessions reflected the uneasy attempt of the regime to hold them in check while retaining the support of the population. Where the Europeans were forced out by the Japanese, as in much of the rest of Asia, there was a determination that colonial rule should not be restored. Armed struggle was not the only method used by national movements, as India shows, but where the colonial regime has already been overthrown by the Japanese (just as in Europe, where old regimes had been overthrown by German or Italian invasion), it was an inevitable form of political response.

Guerilla warfare is not only favoured by the conditions of general total war; it can be seen as a particular variant of total war in itself. Modern guerilla forces should be viewed as states-in-the-process-of-becoming, which indeed is how most of them actually see themselves. Like other states involved in all-out war – indeed more so, since they typically have to compensate for lacking the technical apparatus of their more established enemies – they depend on mobilising the economy and population of the areas which they control. Moreover, nearly all the main guerilla-based revolutionary movements – including those of China, Vietnam, Yugoslavia and Albania – originated in the Stalinised Communist movement of the 1930s and were therefore politically monolithic and totalitarian in tendency. The military method of revolutionary struggle which they chose confirmed this political outlook, since it required a centralism of command and gave little scope for the niceties of democracy or pluralism. Guerilla movements generally ended up creating versions of the Stalinist party-state, although more independent both internally and externally than those of Eastern Europe which were created as a result of Soviet military control.

Although guerilla war continues to be an important form of revolutionary struggle in many parts of the world, there is much to suggest that it belongs to a phase of total war which has long passed in the Northern industrialised world and is slowly dying elsewhere. Guerilla warfare widely occurred in industrialised European states only under the conditions of the Second World War. Since nuclear weapons have outmoded the 1939-45 model of total war, they have almost certainly removed, simultaneously, the prospect of any wide-spread revival of guerilla struggle. In states with democratic traditions or prospects, guerilla struggle, even against repress-ive dictatorships, has ultimately been subordinated to political action. This could be seen in France and Italy in 1945, and in the struggle against the Iberian dictatorships in the 1960s and 1970s. Guerilla forces exist in European democracies only among national minorities such as the Nationalist population in Ulster and the Basques in Northern Spain; these forces too have found it necessary to seek political influence. Pure guerilla struggle, in these conditions, risks isolation from all but a small minority of the population. The ultimate fate of the guerilla is that of the urban terrorist, able to provoke the state to strengthen its repressive apparatus but impotent to achieve his or her own goals.

Guerilla struggle is much more alive in the Third World, but here too its heyday is past. The national movements released by the Second World War were eventually recog-nised by most of the European colonial powers, so that many territories were able to come to political independence without prolonged armed struggle. The Indian case proved more relevant than the Chinese as a general model for much of Asia and Africa after the Second World War. By the late 1960s, the national independence movement had largely achieved its aims, although armed struggle was necessary for the belated victory of national forces in Angola and Mozam-bique and, of course, in Vietnam.

Guerilla action remains an option against repressive national regimes supported by major powers. The Cuban revolution of 1959 made it popular in Latin America in the late 1960s, inspired by Che Guevara, but led to general defeats. Guerilla struggle broke out again in the 1970s in Central America, with a prolonged stalemate in El Salvador and revolutionary success in Nicaragua. Now the US sustains counter-revolutionary guerillas against the Sandinista regime. Elsewhere, it is practised in remote and backward conditions by the liberation movements fighting the Soviet-backed

Ethiopian regime and by the resistance to the Soviet occupation of Afghanistan. It helped bring Mugabe to power in Zimbabwe. It is a method of the Palestinian Liberation Organisation and the African National Congress (South Africa), but both, for different reasons, may have reduced their reliance on it. In these two crucial cases, guerilla action ('terrorism') has to be weighed against other means – diplomacy and, in South Africa, mass action of the black population – as a method of struggle.

Guerilla warfare will remain as long as there are repressive regimes in countries where isolated rural or mountainous regions allow revolutionary forces to survive; but it will never again be a general method of revolutionary change, as it was in 1939-45. China was the classic case, and there will no more be another China – even on the smaller scale of Vietnam or Cuba – than there will be a repeat of the Russian Revolution of 1917. Both revolutionary models, whatever echoes they still evoke, belong to a phase of total war whose time has passed.

4

The Politics of Total War II: Rise and Fall of the Military–Democratic State

The first phase of total war produced situations in which a classical model of socialist revolution would briefly flourish: the second generated, as social historians of war have frequently demonstrated, the conditions for a particular model of social reform. Both variants of socialism were, of course, available as strategies long before the full unfolding of the total war–society relationship. Each was presented, in the classical debates over 'reform and revolution', as dependent on socio-economic relationships. And yet the processes of total war were necessary to bring variants of first the revolutionary, and then the reformist model into being. This is hardly a good advertisement for the explanatory powers of socialist theory, which in none of its early forms really began to grasp the forces which would prove most powerful in shaping socialism in the twentieth century.

Just as the war-society relationships which produced proletarian revolutions in the first phase of total war were to further transform revolutionary politics in the second phase, so the decisive experiences of social reform in this phase were anticipated in very significant ways by earlier developments. Parliamentary democracy itself, with mass political parties – as opposed to parliamentary systems with limited suffrage based on property – only developed in a number of Western societies towards the end of the nineteenth century. This development is widely recognised as reflecting the impact of the industrial working class, and the recognition by capitalist political forces of the need to incorporate it into the political system. The period was one in which mass trade unionism, on the one hand, and a mass circulation press, on the other, first appeared. The development of parliamentary democracy is more often related to these pressures than to preparations for total war. And yet the development of a disciplined mass industrial workforce *also*, from the point of view of the state, made potentially possible the creation of disciplined mass armies. The development of state bureaucracy to administer a more complex industrial society was also the creation of an infrastructure for mass military mobilisation. The growth of press and parties, viewed as new means of mass social control, was also the growth of new means of patriotic, militaristic ideological diffusion.

It is not necessary to argue that mass parliamentary democracy was a product of mass militarism. The point is rather that since industrial capitalism developed within a framework of competing states, it inevitably had profound effects on the prospects for war. Virtually every aspect of the development of capitalism, from the rapid advance of technology, transport and communications to the evolution of new class forces and the political and ideological responses to them, had a major military significance. To adopt the traditional sociological terminology, social changes had both the socio-economic functions which were 'manifest' to contemporaries and social theorists, and military functions which were much more 'latent'.

Mass militarism can be seen, as it was for example by Karl Liebknecht in 1907, as the form of warfare appropriate to capitalism. But there is also a sense in which industrial capitalism and parliamentary democracy were the social and political forms required by a new form of state militarism. In the late nineteenth and early twentieth centuries it was clear that both political nationalism and direct military needs would have social implications. Imperialism begat social reform; the inadequacy of the labour supplied to the armed forces (for example, in Britain during the South African war) stimulated concern at the health and diet of the working class. Warfare had always had implications for welfare, but at the beginning of the twentieth century it was a recognisable motor for change. The First World War greatly accelerated this change, particularly by expanding expectations among working people themselves – expectations which were to be disappointed in the aftermath of the war.

'Participation' in total war

It is tempting to see the period 1914-45, as Mann has done, as a period of 'citizen wars' characterised by a dialectic of wartime participation and the expansion of citizenship (with the decades before 1914 as the social preparation for this military process).[1] As is always the case, however, wide-ranging international experience cannot easily be encompassed by a single category. The actual processes were complex – and contradictory. The First World War did not, directly, produce the extinction of democracy which most revolutionary Marxists predicted at the time. Despite wartime repression, parliamentary democracy became fuller and more widespread in the aftermath of the war. More states were republics; more had universal or quasi-universal suffrage (if only for men and restricted groups of women). The social demands provoked by the war continued to be fought over in post-war politics.

Yet the extension of democracy, both in political and social terms, was extremely precarious. The chief reason for this was of course economic instability: vast social needs could not be met in a world market system whose inadequacies had been deepened rather than overcome by the results of the war. The socio-political potential of mass militarism was, as we have seen, as much revolutionary as reformist. The war generated a dialectic of revolution and counter-revolution; parliamentary democracy in crucial states, notably Italy and Germany, was a fragile compromise imposed on the initial defeat of social revolution, and sooner or later to be overturned in a fuller victory of the counter-revolution. Any virtuous dialectic of citizen rights and warfare was largely overtaken by a much more vicious relationship between totalitarianism and remilitarisation. True, Hitler and Stalin could boast full employment and some forms of welfare, and in Germany living standards were maintained; but these rulers did not offer citizenship, only (at best) the perks awarded to obedient slaves.

The social changes resulting from wartime participation thus varied markedly, within both world wars, as Marwick's comparative study suggests.[2] War unleashed not one but several conflicting sets of social and political processes. To explain these really requires analysis on two levels: the general processes of the mode of warfare and the specific forms which they produced in national societies. The mode of warfare envelops a large number of states: to the extent that they are fighting, or preparing to fight, each other, they are governed by common imperatives of technology, strategy and military organisation, and also of economic and political mobilisation. But each state brings to these relationships its own particular economic strength, geopolitical interests, political system and military tradition. The national experiences result from the interaction of these national state characteristics with the mode of warfare: competition influences the competitors, not least in the actual experience of war by both armies and societies.

Although we are accustomed to thinking of the two world wars as two experiences of total war, the mode of warfare was undergoing rapid development both within and between the two wars. Some of the changes we have already discussed: the expansion of state mobilisation capacities from the *ad hoc* constructions of 1914-18 to the better planned and more comprehensive activities of 1939-45; and the politicisation of total war as a result of the revolutionary and counter-revolutionary developments which issued from the First World War. Equally important and interacting with these political-economic changes were, however, the specific military-technological and strategic changes. These were just as much the product of the experience of the first war. The land stalemate of the trenches had, after all, stimulated the two technological developments – the tank and the bomber – which were to dominate the course of the Second World War. Combined with the advance of statisation and the politicisation of warfare, these produce the main characteristics of the second phase of total war.

Technology and strategy

Since we have discussed at some length the political-economic processes, it is important to comment on the role of the technical dynamic. The industrialisation of warfare is, in a sense, the most fundamental of all the processes of total war: the development of the military 'forces of production'. And yet its role depends on the 'social relations' of militarism, and changes over time. Industrialisation is the most obvious military development of the nineteenth century, and has been well described by writers such as McNeill and Pearton.[3] And yet the most striking product of military industrialisation, the modern warship – on which the greatest economic resources were lavished before 1914 – ultimately proved less crucial to warfare than other less impressive and costly developments. The First World War was dominated by labour-intensive mass militarism, by millions of soldiers armed with guns and shells produced by millions of munitions workers. No matter that the form of warfare they produced resulted in the appalling stalemate of the Western Front: neither battleships, nor the gas, planes and tanks which were introduced during the war could shift the dominance of a more simple, perhaps essentially nineteenth century, kind of war.

If the First World War remained to the end a war of attrition between millions, and the Second World War could not dispense with similar millions of foot soldiers, nevertheless the balance shifted sharply between the two. Although one of the main technical developments – chemical and biological warfare – lurked in the background and was never widely used, tanks and bombers were, as we have seen, central to the war's methods. The Second World War saw rapid improvements in guns, tanks, planes and submarines, and depended much more on the technical changes which were being made and the strategic uses to which they were put. During the war, of course, the most important single military research project ever was carried out, producing the atomic bomb for the Americans in 1945.

The role of technical development depended, we have suggested, on its social context: both broadly socio-economic and more narrowly military-political. No single set of processes within total war, however dynamic, can be seen as decisive in isolation. It is the interaction of technology with strategy, politics and economics which counts. Nevertheless, military technology has proved an increasingly critical instrument. The ability to mass produce guns and shells, means of transportation, and later tanks and planes, was what enabled states to maintain massive armies in the field. Once this was possible, it was inevitable, in any serious war, that it would be done: and so, with the development of the means of total war, there followed its social and economic organisation. Once, then, societies and economies became incorporated into the supply side of war, it was strategically rational – however socially or morally dangerous – to break down the distinction between combatants and civilians, and to seek to attack the socio-economic infrastructure of the enemy. Again, however, the means (primarily aerial bombardment) had to be developed to accomplish this transition.

There were, of course, crucial political and ideological processes involved in this evolution of warfare. It is arguable that some of them were already well set long before the industrialisation of war. Even in the Middle Ages, civilians were frequently regarded as part of the enemy, and later the ideology of the nation had provided a modern basis for this idea. Yet it is not difficult to see that modern arms and methods of military organisation facilitated the abandonment of long compromised 'standards' of warfare. In the First World War, national ideologies easily allowed civilian deaths to be seen as legitimate – even if enemy civilians were not so widely or deliberately attacked as in 1939–45. Total conflict of states and peoples and increasingly absolute means of killing produced such slaughter, in 1914–18, that indiscriminate death came to seem normal. The disenchantment with war, as a result of this experience, might have produced a decisive reaction. But the war also gave rise to totally opposed political systems, and so provided renewed justification for war, even with what was then known of its consequences.

It is characteristic of the second phase of total war, therefore, that while the technical dynamic was greatly accelerated, political polarisation also reached an extreme. The relationship between these two processes is central to understanding both the general features of this phase and the different national experiences. At a general level, the combination of politics and military technology meant that attacking civilian population centres, not merely as economic targets but because of their significance for political morale, became a 'normal' feature of warfare. The escalation of this strategy, initiated by Germany, became a central feature of Allied activity. It culminated in Europe in the fire-bombing of Dresden, which was of neither major military nor economic significance, only months before the final defeat of Hitler. This development explains why the atomic bomb, with its enormous enhancement of the capability for indiscriminate killing, could so easily be used against Japan. The strategic choices which undermined possible moral objections had already been made at lower levels of weaponry. The awesome new atomic technology simply carried forward the strategic and political lines already established. Only after the bomb was dropped did the new issues which it raised slowly begin to be perceived.

Absolute political polarisation permitted the large-scale indiscriminate killing of civilians, which military technology made possible, in the Second World War. For governments and peoples, there was little possible qualification of the politics of the struggle; whatever was militarily necessary – and strategic, even atomic bombing could certainly be presented as necessary, however much we may argue with hindsight – was politically justifiable. This same combination of total politics and murderous technology was involved in the Nazis' extermination policies. The difference was that killing, here, was the direct realisation of a political goal, not a sordid military means to an altogether more praiseworthy politics. The distinction is there, but it is not always as clear in practice as it appears in theory and apologia. Certainly the exterminist politics of Nazism adapted the increasingly exterminist military means of total war to its particular ends. But the bureaucratic efficiency of the extermination process belonged to the methodology of modern total war. As we have already suggested, it is not easy to explain it outside the context of the Second World War.

National experiences of the Second World War

The second phase of total war differed from the first in that mass politics increasingly displaced more traditional definitions of state interests, and that qualitative changes in military technology and strategy started to displace sheer quantities of men and munitions as critical factors. The transition can be seen as one from *labour-intensive, nationalistic mass militarism* to *technologically and politically enhanced mass militarism*. During the Second World War, we were still in the epoch of mass armies, but rapid technological (as well as political) changes had taken place which produced a quite different war. The second phase has much more in common with the first than with the coming third (nuclear) phase, but there are clear lines of development within it which anticipate the more radical transformation of the years after 1945.

National experience of the phases of total war is enormously varied. Most fundamentally, it depends on economic development: no state can participate in modern warfare without at least some of the necessary elements of population, industry, state organisation, etc. And yet there is nothing like a one-to-one correspondence between economic strength, or level of economic development, and military capacity. The Tsar mobilised his peasants in 1914, only 50 years out of serfdom, to compete with the armies of industrialised Western Europe. The Chinese Communists mobilised their peasants against the industrial might of Imperial Japan. Both struggles reflected their economic base: Tsarist Russia eventually broke under the strain, while the Chinese alone could not defeat the Japanese. In both world wars too, the industrial might of the USA ultimately played a decisive role; and Soviet industrialisation, for all its costs, was a necessary foundation for the Soviet Union's historic role in defeating Nazism. It was at least very unlikely that the Axis powers could ever have withstood the combined weight of the Allied economies in a prolonged war. This, after all, was why Hitler tried to rely on *Blitzkrieg*.

While economic strength is the foundation of military capacity, it is no more than this, and everything depends on how it is used. The state which makes its military commitments a higher priority may be the military equal of an economically stronger state; and, in any case, major wars are intersecting contests of a group of alliances rather than individual states. The actual outcome of war, moreover, can hardly be read off from the disposition of military – still less economic – forces at its outset. In military terms, as strategists have indicated, the interaction of policy, strategy and supply is crucial. In the end there is no substitute for understanding the processes of war itself, culminating, as Clausewitz argued, in the experience of battle. But battle, in total war, is no longer something which takes place apart from society, involving only professional armed forces. The armed forces are drawn, through conscription, from the entire society; society experiences war both indirectly, through economic and political mobilisation, and directly, as centres of population are systematically fought over on land and in the air.

Battle in total war takes many forms, some of which – at sea, in deserts and remote jungles, etc. – are in isolated 'battlefields' but many of which – aerial bombardment and some tank advances, for example – are actually concentrated on civilian centres. The transition from the first to the second phase of total war is crucial here. The 'home front', which in 1914-18 was largely an economic and political arena, became in 1939-45 much more of a real military 'front'. On the one hand this was because, especially in continental Europe, the shifting land battlefield engulfed successive societies and regions. On the other hand, it was because the major combatants' hinterlands, the true 'home fronts' inaccessible to land attack, became aerial targets. Here is the real convergence of the social and military logic of total war.

National experiences of total war have largely been encompassed by sociologists and social historians under the rubric of the 'Military Participation Ratio' (MPR) thesis. First advanced by Andreski as part of an ambitious comparative sociology of military organisation, it suggests that a crucial factor in the effect of war on society is the proportion of a society's members who are mobilised in its armed forces.[4] In the more grounded historical work of Marwick, this formula is modified to suggest that 'wartime' rather than, in the strict sense, 'military' participation is the key. Although Marwick's comparative study shows a full awareness of the varied forms of civilian participation and their social effects in different national contexts, his earlier popular study of Britain helped to crystallise a particular sense of wartime participation.[5] In line with other studies of Britain in the Second World War, the society is seen as one in which the active participation of citizens in wartime struggle resulted in a major process of social reform. Mann has gone further, seeing this as a general tendency of 'the period of citizen wars' (1914-45). Such wars, he argues, while characterised by great attrition, destruction and draining of public resources, and hence 'irrational as a means to the stated ends' are nevertheless 'rational as a contribution to citizen well-being'.[6]

The general concept of civilian 'participation' requires some discussion before we look at the British case in comparative perspective. The term 'participation' is open to weak (neutral) and strong (positively evaluated) meanings. The population always participates in total war in the sense that it is mobilised, used, forced to work, fight and die for the state. It does not always participate in the sense of being able to influence the aims and conduct of the war, or of enhancing its post-war influence on social and economic organisation or its post-war social rights. Total war is at its very best a two-way process, in which the state coerces the population but the population endorses its own coercion and thereby improves its position in and influence on the state. At its worst, as in the cases of Nazi Germany, Imperial Japan and Stalinist Russia – whatever their popular appeal or temporary economic benefits they offered – all significant rights are denied, and only coercion remains.

It seems wrong to see these negative cases, as Mann has done, as exceptions in this period of militarism. On the contrary, they are organic products of the second phase of total war, with its political polarisation, and represent major models of mass militarism. While, on the assumption that the USA was bound to enter the war, it may be argued that the Western democracies were bound to be victorious, this smacks of the complacency of hindsight. The totalitarian models of war-mobilisation *could* have been successful, and if they had, the outcome of the Second World War would have been unprecedented darkness. Orwell, after all, saw *1984* coming despite the victory of the democracies, and he was right to the extent that the subsequent decades have seen a continuing problem of authoritarianism in Western democratic states. With a different outcome in 1945, he would neither have needed, nor been able, to write the book: a close approximation to his nightmare would already have been reality. Such a world would doubtless have contained its own contradictions, economic as well as political and military, but it would have been a very different conclusion to the period of total war.

The post-1945 economic and political systems were therefore the result of the victory of particular military forces, representing particular forms of wartime mobilisation. The main victors were the United States, Britain and their allies, which were able to assist forces favouring parliamentary democratic states to restore or create such institutions, and with them pro-American governments, in Japan and most Western European societies. The secondary victor was the Soviet Union, which was able to manoeuvre to bring about Soviet-type states in all the Eastern European countries it occupied. Local victors such as the Yugoslav, Albanian and Chinese Communists were able to create states according to their own models (the Chinese only after further revolutionary struggle).

The dialectic of wartime participation and post-war change was muffled in most of the occupied countries by the role of the new occupiers, the victorious Allies. In Western Europe, local resistance forces who had fought against Nazi occupation did have some part in the post-war order, but radical left-wing movements were either defeated by force of arms (as in Greece) or inhibited from pressing their claims by Stalin's agreement with the US and Britain (as in Italy and France). By the late 1940s, left-wing parties were manoeuvred out of government even in countries where the Resistance had been strong. The forces which survived to dominate the state were those sections of the Right not tainted by collaboration with fascism, such as Gaullists and Christian Democrats. The Communist parties consolidated their right to be the main forces of opposition in Italy and France. In the defeated countries, especially Germany and Japan, the post-war order was erected within the firm constraints imposed by the occupying Allies, and handed over to leaders of whom they approved.

In Eastern Europe, moreover, the dialectic of resistance

and post-war change was even weaker. The Soviet Union was careful not to rest its control on leaders who had a national base. In Poland, for example, the Red Army had not entered the capital until after the defeat of the Warsaw Uprising, thus ensuring that it did not have to share power with the heroes of a national revolt. Where the Communist Party had some real support, notably in Czechoslovakia, the Soviet Union ensured that the party leaders relied for their positions on Moscow rather than the working class. There, as elsewhere, it was Moscow Communists rather than those with a local base who inherited the post-war state and eliminated their non-Communist rivals.

The consolidation of parliamentary democracy in most Western states rested more, then, on the international balance of military, political and economic power than on the strength of popular forces. The extension of democratic rights to include social rights, and the subsequent development of a welfare apparatus in most countries, were the result of a number of factors other than the wartime participation of the population. Important among these were the central role necessarily taken by states in the immediate post-war reconstruction; the ideology of planning and intervention which had been strengthened by wartime experience; and the elimination of much of the traditional right because of its associations with fascism. Most crucial of all, though, was probably the development of new economic conditions. Reconstruction generated a boom, boosted by Korean War rearmament in the US, Britain and elsewhere, which created seemingly permanent full employment. Social reform in most Western countries was not therefore, as in Britain, an immediate consequence of war. On the contrary, the early post-war years in most of continental Europe and Japan were years of great hardship and desperate reconstruction measures. Social reform only developed in conditions of full employment in the 1950s: instead of being implemented by left-wing parties, it was often carried through by the new moderate forces of the Right which benefited from the boom.

The character of post-war states certainly depended in large part on societies' experience of war: but not according to a single pattern of wartime participation and social reform. At this point it is important to stress the variety of national experiences in the Second World War. Of course, the condition in which societies entered the war is also important. Economically, they ranged from the advanced capitalisms of North America, Western Europe and Australasia; through the less industrially developed societies of Japan, the Soviet Union and Southern and Eastern Europe; to the largely peasant societies of China, India and the rest of Asia and the Middle East. Politically, they were sharply divided between parliamentary democracies, fascist, Stalinist and other authoritarian regimes. Actual war experience interacted with the different bases provided by socio-economic relations and political institutions.

National war-experiences in 1939-45 offer an immense range. Although this was a 'world war', some parts of the world were not directly involved. Most of Latin America was neutral, and it has been argued that important economic and political developments stemmed from its relative isolation; much of Africa, belonging to the colonial empires of the European combatants, was only indirectly involved, although the war stimulated movements for national independence. In Asia, the war was fought with murderous intensity from China south to the East Indies, and from India eastwards to the Pacific. In countries occupied by Japan, Communist and other nationalist resistance forces flourished and after the war eventually brought about the liquidation of the colonial states. In India, which stood in a similar relation to the war in Asia as did Britain to the war in Europe, the war effort of the Raj gave a new impetus to the Congress's drive to independence. Its eventual, but qualified, success – and the almost uniquely long-lived parliamentary system which resulted from it – are testimony to something like the 'wartime participation' effect which can be seen in Britain. Elsewhere in Asia, however, where the war more directly ravaged society, post-war political developments took more drastic forms: from the successful revolutionary struggles of the Chinese and (after 30 years' further war against France and the US) the Vietnamese Communists; to various authoritarian nationalisms such as those of Malaysia, Indonesia and Burma.

In the industrialised and semi-industrialised states of North America, Europe, Japan, Australasia and South Africa, the range of war experience was, if anything, even wider. At one extreme the United States (after the trauma of Pearl Harbor), Canada, Australia, New Zealand and South Africa experienced little or nothing that resembled direct attack on their societies. North America in particular was never in much danger of invasion: its people participated in a war that was comfortably across the oceans. The main cost was the loss of American lives in far-flung theatres of war. For the people at home, the Second World War brought an unprecedented economic boom. War expenditure abolished unemployment, drove forward economic growth, and saw a rapid increase in real living standards. The American Left, which had prospered in the New Deal period and the labour struggles of the 1930s, advanced further during the war and its immediate aftermath. But overall the left was still marginal, and there was relatively weak pressure for social reform in a society where private affluence had grown so markedly. The Cold War and Senator McCarthy put paid to the modest momentum for social advances which resulted from the war years.

There is an overwhelming contrast between the European and North American experiences. Most of continental Europe was fought over and much of it was devastated. Nevertheless, the experiences involved were extremely varied. For the Jews of Eastern Europe, 'wartime participation' ultimately meant their systematic extermination. The Poles, Russians, Ukrainians, and other peoples of the western Soviet Union, despite contrasting political positions with regard to the war, shared a common pattern of appalling misery, brutal occupation, and massive loss of life. By comparison, the peoples of Western Europe suffered much milder forms of occupation; the Nazis followed their racial theories to prefer Western Europeans, especially Aryans, to Slavs and Jews. There was great hardship and repression, but the death toll was very modest by comparison with the East. The Germans stood, of course, at the centre of these contrasting experiences – at the height of their success, commanding an empire of huge extremes. As the German people prospered in the early part of the war, with the Reich victorious and only modest inroads into their relatively comfortable living standards, so of course they suffered from the mass bombing and eventual disintegration of their economy in the later years. The Nazis' war first offered real advantages to many Germans (although, even more than the ultimately victorious Americans, the conquering Germans had to lose enormous numbers of soldiers). But in the end it left their society devastated. A similar pattern was followed in Japan.

In the range of war experiences, from the unprecedented slaughter of civilians in Eastern Europe to the war boom in the US, Britain's experience stands out as unique. Britain stood, in terms of the intensity of civilian deaths, danger and hardship as well as in its geographical position, between occupied Western Europe and secure North America. Unlike most of Europe, Britain was never occupied or defeated. Unlike the other major European protagonists, Britain experienced mass mobilisation under a parliamentary democracy rather than fascist or Stalinist totalitarianism. But unlike (for the most part) the white dominions and the US, Britain's democratic mobilisation occurred under conditions of real hardship and direct physical threat.

The uniqueness of British war experience lies in the combination of a real but unrealised threat of invasion, real but relatively limited civilian casualties and hardship, and a process of democratic mobilisation. British society was threatened, and suffered, enough to have radicalising social effects; but not so much as to lead to invasion, defeat or the sort of devastation and killing which left the people of Eastern and Central Europe (and much of Asia) so desperate in 1945. Post-war British democracy was forged as a result of a severe test of state and society, in which the state directly mobilised society and society was in turn able to secure (within a short period after the end of the war) major reforms in the state. But there was continuity in the state, in the maintenance of modestly adequate living standards, and in the working-class movement. The British post-war 'settlement' was an adaptation of existing parliamentary institutions to the demands for social reform generated in the population as a result of the war effort. The post-war Labour government was headed by Attlee, who had been Deputy Prime Minister in charge of the 'home front' for five years: this symbolised not just the social-democratic bias of the settlement, but the continuity with the framework of social policy and participation generated by the war.

Britain is therefore an *exceptionally* strong case of what Mann calls 'the dialectic of development of civic and military participation'.[7] Everywhere, in the aftermath of the Second World War, the state's role was greatly enhanced: the wartime accumulation of powers led directly into the mammoth task of post-war reconstruction. In every industrialised state that fell under the control of the Western democracies, some form of parliamentary democracy was established. Equally, in an era of planning and reconstruction, the state everywhere concerned itself more than ever before with the health, education, welfare and economic security of its citizens. (This was also true of Eastern Europe, where political rights, although legally established, had little practical meaning.) Although the role of the resistance in many countries ensured that the state form was not simply imposed by the Allies and the ruling groups which they fostered, only in Britain were democratic forms extended as a direct consequence of wartime participation. This meant, first, that Britain had a formally more complete 'welfare state' than most other countries: only Australia and New Zealand (whose war experience is most closely analogous to Britain's) and the Scandinavian countries provide rough comparisons. But, more crucially than that, although some other countries might match Britain's welfare system (and in terms of standards, many eventually surpassed it), it meant that in Britain the 'welfare state' rested on exceptional, unique wartime foundations.

Most post-war parliamentary democracies combined considerable political and socio-economic democratisation with a concentration of military, political and ideological power in state structures defined by emerging international alignments. In a few, traditional non-alignment or post-war geopolitics meant formal neutrality in the new conflict between the two parts of a divided continent: such states have paid their respects to the realities of power, and have maintained their own very considerable armaments. In most states, however, post-war conflicts have meant military and political incorporation into the Atlantic Alliance. State institutions have been formed around these fundamental commitments, involving generally very substantial military forces and expenditures. The realities of East–West conflict have meant that military institutions have retained a major weight in most states, despite the extension of democracy.

In this sense, all post-1945 democracies can be described as 'military-democratic' states. In the United States, where the most striking period of welfare state advance was in the 1930s, the post-war years are most notable for the build-up of military power. C. Wright Mills suggested that the military had become one of the three constituents of the US power elite.[8] The precise weight to be assigned to the military, compared to the political and economic elites, may be controversial. What is undoubtedly true, regardless of whether it is the political or military elite which exercises power, is that military issues and decisions have become central to it. As the US has become dominant in the world order, and as nuclear weapons have centralised military decision-making, so a higher level of power has undoubtedly crystallised to which only a few have access.

In Western European states, which have lost their global pre-eminence since 1945, the *movement* may be in a different direction from that of the US. Compared to the uncertain democracy of the inter-war years, the democratic gains have been real, both in political and socio-economic terms. But, as suggested above, the defining character of international military realities makes the military commitments of states dominate all social goals. In this sense, European states can still usefully be described as military-democratic. The importance of this dual description is that it indicates an ongoing source of tensions in the state, between its external commitments and the social forces which may be active in its internal democratic space.

Among Western military-democratic states, Britain is one in which both sides of the modern state form are exceptionally developed. On the one hand, Britain is, in consequence of its junior partnership in the victory of 1945, a member of NATO with military importance disproportionate to its declining economic and political roles. Britain has had military expenditure at a consistently higher level than any other European NATO state (or Japan); indeed this is one explanation put forward for Britain's economic decline.[9] On the other hand, British democracy has not only a long history, uninterrupted by invasion or dictatorship; it has been almost uniquely reinforced by the social consequences of war participation. But this over-determination of the military-democratic state in Britain also means that it has become unusually vulnerable to the conflicts inherent in its structure.

The argument that the framework of post-war democracy is limited and contradictory has been widely advanced: as Stuart Hall has put it, the Keynesian Welfare State 'is a contradictory structure, a "historic compromise", which both achieved something in a reformist direction for the working class *and* became an instrument for disciplining it'.[10] What has largely been missed in discussions of this contradiction is how far it was the product of wartime mobilisation. 'Democracy' in wartime issued from above: the government, and 'experts' such as Keynes and Beveridge whose ideas and reports helped to shape the desired better society, were the sources of initiatives. They responded to what they perceived as the demands of the people, and to feedback from them, but there was very limited scope for direct popular initiatives. Participation – the ambiguity of the term has already been noted – did not mean direct democracy from the bottom. The state, which was centralised for war, remained centralised for the peace. Indeed, social reform was largely a matter of converting the wartime planning machine to the problems of peace. Democracy consisted in the expectations of, and support for, this development which undoubtedly existed in the majority of the population, rather than in direct mass involvement.

The post-war Labour government was noted for its centralist, bureaucratic methods. These have often been ascribed to the statist ideology of Fabianism, or Labourism, but ideology alone cannot explain them. The working-class movement had, after all, other ideological traditions. The 'selection' of a statist ideology reflected the general advance of the state in society between – and even more during – the wars. The centralism of welfare-state social democracy, with its concepts of nationalisation and bureaucratic planning, issued from the centralism of the war-state and war-economy. Its contradictions were the contradictions of Second World War democratic militarism: between the imperatives of control and mass manipulation by a secretive centralised state, and the democratic, reform-based input of mass participation. The tension was largely controlled, during the actual war years and the immediate aftermath, although popular expectations did sometimes run ahead of state action. It gradually became fully apparent, and finally developed into a fundamental cleavage, in the late post-war period. The war-state has become a target for both grassroots democratisers on the left and economic libertarians on the right.

The context of military participation has widely been seen as fundamental to the social changes of the war and immediate post-war period. They are well served by social and political historians such as Calder and Addison, as well as by the more sociologically explicit work of Marwick.[11] The problem arises with the main post-war period (that contemporary Britain is still, 40 years later, defined in relation to wartime experience says much about its centrality). Here the military context becomes, necessarily, less total and less visible, and tends to be almost wholly replaced by the socio-economic issues which are, obviously, at the front of the stage. Social historians of military participation have not carried their analyses seriously into the longer post-war term: even a writer such as Middlemas, who recognises the centrality of war in earlier periods, neglects the military context in his account of socio-economic change. Similarly sociologists concerned with the problems of political power and the decline of consensus, as a sample of otherwise excellent recent British textbooks shows, define these almost completely without reference to the context of military power.[12] Here social theory clearly lags behind social consciousness, for since 1979 international and military issues have been central to the problems of the state in Britain and other Western societies.

What is proposed here, then, is a double revision of existing historical and sociological interpretations. On the one hand, the social theory of military participation, which has been qualified as a general theory of wartime experience, should nevertheless be *extended* so that we may examine its relevance to the post-war period. On the other hand, it is suggested that almost all historical and sociological writing, not least Marxist-influenced writing, has neglected a fundamental dimension of the processes of socio-economic and political change in Britain since 1945. Unless we see Britain at that point as something like a 'military-democratic' state, we cannot chart its subsequent mutation.

It is not difficult to see the early post-war reforms as belonging essentially to the period of wartime mobilisation. This is not to deny the political role of Labour reformism which, as Morgan has emphasised, took the wartime coalition's welfare proposals significantly further.[13] But Labour's dominance was itself a product of the wartime period. In political terms, the war-mobilisation period can be seen as lasting until about 1947, by which time most of Labour's main reforms had either been achieved, or at least launched. The year 1947 was one of crisis for the government, and was marked internationally by the onset of the Cold War (although the origins of this went back to US–Soviet rivalry in the later stages of the war).

The decade after 1947 can be seen as one of transition from the politics of war mobilisation to the politics of the nuclear age. In this decade, despite military and economic demobilisation from the unprecedented levels of 1939-45, Britain remained within the mould cast for it by the war. Economically, it retained the appearance of a major power, while most of Western Europe and Japan were concerned with fundamental reconstruction. Politically, Britain was still undisputably one of the great powers, a major actor in the Cold War era – even if its inferiority to the superpowers was there for all to see. Militarily, early 1947 also saw the beginnings of Britain's atomic bomb, the ultimate expression of the Labour government's belief in Britain's status. But this programme – which remained secret until after Churchill returned to power in 1951 – was at this stage only an addition to Britain's military capabilities, which were still based on a Second World War kind of militarism. The Korean war saw massive conventional rearmament; the armed forces remained based on conscription (for the first time outside war); and a comprehensive system of civil defence stayed in place.

The period from about 1947 to 1957 was marked, then, by a modified version (obviously much less intense outside actual total war) of the Second World War model of military participation. Presided over by its wartime leaders (Attlee, Churchill, Eden), there was a continuation of the wartime consensus on two fundamental bases. The first of these was the widely recognised economic and social 'settlement' of the welfare state, full employment and economic intervention. The second, less often acknowledged by recent writers but equally essential, was the political–military framework of the Atlantic Alliance, Britain's world role and continuing national mobilisation. Where 'democracy versus fascism' had once provided the ideological cement, it was now 'democracy versus Communism'. This was the era of Cold War conformity, as stifling in Britain as it was threatening in the US.

Korea marked the high point of this phase, and also the point at which it was clearest that the Cold War polarisation blocked off further social advance. Suez was its *denouement*, showing that it was no longer possible for Britain to continue as a great power in the old way. The following year, under Macmillan, came a fundamental reassessment of Britain's military policies, recognising the supremacy of nuclear weapons and marking the beginning of the end for the 1939-45 model of military participation. Conscription was to be ended, defence spending reduced, and instead there was a reliance on the 'independent nuclear deterrent'. This was followed by moves to demobilise civil defence, and in 1968 by its virtual disbandment.

The changing basis of 'defence' marked the beginning of the end for Britain's 'military–democratic' state. From 1957 onwards, the military establishment became more and more separate, and ultimately almost invisible, from the people. The state recognised that it would dispense with the people in a future nuclear war; it had largely dispensed with the pretence of involving them in war-preparation, too. The secret, capital-intensive part of the state's military power was to be developed; the people were not expected to discuss or decide, but merely to give their passive consent. The new policies were not, however, the abandonment of Britain's great power pretensions, but a recognition that they were neither politically viable nor financially affordable on the old basis. The state was opting for the cheaper, symbolic assertion of Britain's continuing military pretensions, rather than the older model of large armies and global reach. 'East of Suez' was finally abandoned, after a further crisis, under the Labour government in the mid-1960s; but the logic had been anticipated a decade earlier.

The explicit recognition of the nuclear age at first provoked an opposition movement. The young who were roused by the Suez fiasco were not likely to embrace a nuclear defence policy. The Campaign for Nuclear Disarmament (CND) brought about the first popular cleavage in the post-war 'consensus'. (Rumblings of opposition to Korean war rearmament, German rearmament and earlier nuclear tests had occurred within the Labour movement, or in small and marginal protest groups.) The first steps to break up the 'military–democratic' consensus were, therefore, met with a mass movement. But this was worn down, defused, and eventually marginalised: after 1964, the issues of nuclear weapons and defence policy were absent from popular radical politics, indeed from national politics generally except in the elite corridors of the defence establishment. The state enjoyed 15 years of virtually complete popular indifference to its military preparations, ended only by the cruise missiles debate at the very end of 1979.

CND laid the foundation for a succession of radical campaigns and protest movements which often focussed on international or domestic issues touching defence or nuclear policy (apartheid, Vietnam, students, Northern Ireland, nuclear power). But despite this continuing radical presence, the central contradictions of the nuclear age appeared (before the 1980s) to be socio-economic. It seemed that the economic growth of the post-war boom had opened up a new phase of class conflict, exacerbated by the onset of recession in the 1970s. Wages and trade union rights, and later inflation, unemployment and the welfare state, were the central issues of British politics. Debates about Britain's military role in general, especially its nuclear-armed core, were so marginal between 1964 and 1979 that it is difficult to credit the idea that military participation can tell us anything significant about the overall trajectory of the British state.

It must be argued, however, that the decline and near-disappearance of a crucial social cement, holding together the post-war social order and the state, is as important as its earlier centrality. Hand in hand with military participation had gone economic and social participation; along with military duty had come economic and social rights. The connection of the two had been central to their general acceptance – in particular to the support of the political right in the Conservative Party for reforms which it had previously considered dangerously left-wing. Wartime participation was, in this sense, essential to the post-war consensus. Even if economic and social participation, as values, achieved a centrality of their own – the core of the consensus coming to be located in state intervention, full employment and the welfare state – they were more easily jettisoned when their underpinning in military participation was gone. The decline of military participation was a necessary, if not a sufficient, condition for the break-up of the consensus.

The disappearance of militarism from public consciousness was not of course its disappearance from society, but a separation of militarism from the sources of social democracy in the broad sense. So long as 'defence' remained a purely elite issue, the consensus on defence could survive, when the socio-economic consensus was already under strain. The final rupture, in 1980-81, was therefore quite dramatic, as soon as a popular challenge to defence policies re-emerged. In May 1979 a Labour government left office, having secretly modernised Polaris, authorised NATO's 3 per cent real increase at a time of welfare cuts, begun negotiations about Trident, and participated in NATO policy discussions on cruise missiles. By January 1981, at its Wembley conference, Labour (in response to the peace movement and the influence of unilateralists in the trade unions) was moving towards a non-nuclear defence policy. In response to this movement, and also to constitutional changes, a section of its right-wing formed the Social Democratic Party. To understand how such fundamental developments could take place so rapidly, we must recognise that the Atlanticist, nuclear consensus of the main parties had long since lost the active basis of ideological support, let alone the real military participation, of its origins.

It rested on a passive, at best routine, acquiescence of the population in the military preparations of the state.

The British state has moved, therefore, from a military–democratic to a nuclear relationship with society. Nuclear weapons have, as C. Wright Mills argued much earlier in the nuclear age, centralised military-political power and reduced democratic politics to the lower rungs of power.[14] Even the ideological dimensions of nuclear rivalry stayed passive in Britain, as in most Western societies, so long as the arms race remained more of a technical than a political conflict. But a regime which is dispensing with much of the consensus socio-economic legitimation of state power needs to emphasise older, more fundamental legitimations: 'law and order' and 'defence'. A good deal has been written, for example by Hall and his colleagues, to indicate the role of 'law and order' issues in the breakdown of the post-war consensus and in the attempt to constitute a new 'authoritarian populist' consensus.[15] 'Defence' issues were not prominent at all, and when first raised by the revived disarmament movement in 1980-81, found no easy answers from ministers and ideologues who had simply not developed a style of politics to deal with the rapid military-technological changes of the arms race.

The re-creation of an ideology of defence in Britain has relied considerably on the basic concept of 'deterrence', deployed against CND a quarter of a century ago, despite all its inherent contradictions and subsequent strategic mutations. In Britain especially, in contrast to other countries in Western Europe, the political argument has often been remarkably crude and unreconstructed. In part this has to do with the simple party and electoral systems within which British politics are conducted. War brought no constitutional reform, only the consolidation of a Labour–Tory two-party system. Equally, however, the crudeness of the argument reflects the weak popular appeal of nuclear defence, and the difficulty of popularising new weapon systems. A good deal of ideological weight has therefore been given, not to Reaganesque pictures of 'evil empires' which would have limited appeal in the British case, but to a military analogy with the situation before the Second World War. The analogy is inevitably extremely simple, since Gorbachev is manifestly not Hitler, and no serious comparison could be drawn between the strategic interests and policies of the Soviet Union today and Nazi Germany. But the Thatcher government clearly needs to appeal to that part of the ideological foundation of the 'military-democratic' state which is available to it; even as it dismantles and disowns the socio-economic content of the post-war settlement.

The ideological residues of military participation were most effectively, if ultimately incongruously, exploited by Thatcher in the Falklands war. As Barnett has argued, the ideological framework of post-war British politics can be traced back to the marriage of Tory-imperialist patriotism and Labourist social reform in the wartime coalition government.[16] This he calls 'Churchillism': the shared ideology of the political elite. Its echoes in the Falklands war were, however, hollow and deformed: myths and symbols lacking in their original substance. The shrill version of national leadership offered by Thatcher lacked the wide base of Churchill's; 'Argy-bashing', while reminiscent of Cold War 'Red-baiting', lacked the foundations of real hatred which were felt for Nazism in the Second World War. Ultimately the explanation for this is the decline of military participation: the Falklands were not an exception, but confirmed the trend. Although the symbols of the Second World War could be applied, as Barnett notes, their practical meaning was fundamentally changed. The Falklands war vindicated small, professional armed forces, acting on behalf of the nation but needing no real mass participation to carry out their tasks. British civilian involvement was little more than that of the tiny Falklands population itself. For the vast majority, it was limited to the utterly passive, vicarious consumption of exceptionally closely filtered news, and the expression of support in the opinion polls. Far from the Falklands representing a renewal of the Second World War type of participation, the war was a perfect demonstration of Mann's division between the 'deterrence-science' militarism of the professional elite and the 'spectator-sport' militarism of the mass. Tens of millions of people in Britain were glued to their TV sets for scanty news of the few thousands tossing in the South Atlantic on their behalf – as clear a picture as one could want of this divide. Britain is therefore, in the late 1980s, a society in which the contradictions of the military–democratic state have been further exposed than in any other – by the development of nuclear militarism. In Britain, above all, it is important that any perspective for social change should be based on understanding the changed character of warfare. Society and state have moved beyond the forms which classical total war created; so, as we contemplate the form which radicalism can take in Britain, we must clearly move beyond the politics of total war.

5
Beyond the Politics of
Total War

We have seen in previous chapters that each of the phases of total war has seen the development of specific radical political forms. The first phase of labour-intensive mass militarism generated revolutionary contradictions, and led to the first successful socialist revolution in Russia. The second phase, in which politicisation and technological development transformed total war, created the conditions in which social reformism could succeed, above all in Britain.

These political forms had different relationships to militarism. Social revolution grew out of the contradictions of mass militarism, and involved revolutionary anti-militarism. The Russian Revolution, as we have seen, can be considered in large part a revolution against militarism, although for the revolutionary leaders this was a conditional stance. Revolutionary anti-militarism gave way to revolutionary militarism as counter-revolution threatened. Social reform, on the other hand, grew out of the bonding together of society and state: it was not anti-militarist in any except the vague sense of wishing to see a peaceful world after the conclusion of the war.

Social revolution and social reform grew, moreover, out of conditions which only developed fully with war itself. Far more radical changes occurred when war was superimposed on social conflict, than in the period of 'peace' or war-preparation. Mass mobilisation created huge social forces, more concentrated than had ever been seen in 'peacetime' capitalism, with a potential for revolt. In Russia in 1917, the soldiers at the front combined with the workers in heavy industry and the munitions factories to create a revolution, with the peasants, too, rising against the sufferings the war imposed. Elsewhere the revolt was more restrained, but it existed: even in Britain, workers organised against the effects of war, while at the front British soldiers were involved in extensive war-avoidance and even in mutinies.[1] None of this led to social revolution, but revolutionary anti-militarist politics developed on the British left during the First World War.[2]

Social reform in the Second World War resulted partly from an awareness of the revolt generated in the first war, the disillusionment at the failure of social reform after it, and the need to overcome the resentments of the depression. Only a much closer socio-political linking of society and state could achieve the mobilisation needed to defeat Nazism. Despite the reform potential of the wartime coalition in Britain, class conflict remained, erupting into industrial struggles towards the end of the war. Nothing like the political anti-militarism of 1914-18 developed, however, since the left, after 1941 at least, was almost united in support of the war.[3]

The third phase of total war utterly transforms the relationship between radical politics and war-resistance. In the first place, social contradictions will hardly play the same sort of role in a nuclear war. If, as seems likely, the war is instantaneously absolute (even NATO scenarios envisage a rapid escalation from a short period of 'tension' to a swift 'conventional' war leading directly to nuclear war), there will be neither the time nor the space for social conflict. By the time nuclear war is even likely, war-resistance may be largely beside the point. The resistance to nuclear war has to be successful in the period of general war-preparation. The key question is the relationship between militarism and anti-militarism, and the wider social struggles of the society in which nuclear war is prepared.

Central to the argument here is that war-resistance in the nuclear age cannot easily be converted into another form of militarism, as happened to revolutionary anti-militarism in the

First World War. The growing historical redundancy of war means that the task is to develop non-military alternatives, rather than different forms of militarism. The development of warfare towards human extermination is irreversible within the terms of war; only by moving beyond them is there any hope.

Nuclear militarism and social participation

The reasons for the development of radical politics in the first two phases of total war were mainly to do with the contradictions of military *participation*. Both the First and Second World Wars involved total societal mobilisation. A nuclear war, however, will mobilise society as a whole only in the sense of Auschwitz, by delivering it to mass destruction. The mobilisation process proper is transferred back into the war-preparation stage: but, as we have seen, nuclear militarism is not mass militarism in the same sense. Small professional armed forces and technologically skilled work forces in the armaments industries 'participate' more or less directly; the mass of society participate mainly in the sense of ideological mobilisation. Even this ideological mobilisation, as an active process, is limited to periods of relative crisis in international relations and the arms race.

The social contradictions of nuclear militarism are therefore very different from those of previous phases of total war. Conflicts within the military sectors of society are limited. Small, relatively well-paid professional armies do not generate revolt in the same way as mass armies of raw conscripts. Skilled arms workers, well aware of their dependence on nuclear militarism, will revolt only if made redundant, although those with trade union traditions may be open to the politics of arms conversion. By and large, however, the military sectors will provide only a flow of individual critics: disillusioned scientists, retired generals, politicised union officials and shop stewards. These are important to an anti-war movement, but they do not provide its basis. The crucial social contradictions of nuclear militarism are therefore those which affect the wider society. In general, these will arise not through anything which can seriously be called 'military participation' but through external or indirect effects. This is because of the remoteness of the nuclear arms race and society.

The arms race is best conceived of as an arch over society: its twin pillars, in the military and the military-industrial sectors, stand on the edges of society. Most members of society live for the majority of the time without being aware that the arch is there, above them, although in fact it is constantly being enlarged, with jagged edges pointing down at them as well as up at 'the enemy'. The arch requires many of the best building materials in society, but most people do not see these being diverted from ordinary social uses.

Only when a particularly sharp international incident or escalation of the arms race occurs do most of society become aware of this overarching military reality. Because the arms race is so abstracted from everyday social life, there is little ongoing social conflict about it. Conflict is confined to various elite interest groups in the armed forces, the state and military industry. Only when extraordinary developments occur (particularly a series of international conflicts and arms race issues, such as coincided at the beginning of the 1980s) is widespread social awareness generated. This, combined with the national political situations prevailing, is also the context in which anti-nuclear weapons movements develop. Not surprisingly, such movements have considerable difficulty in maintaining their momentum.

A cycle of protest actions, even involving millions, may build up over several years, but given the abstractness of nuclear issues it is difficult to achieve concrete results. The first CND movement in Britain did not remove a single missile. The wider European peace movement of the 1980s has contributed to the removal of intermediate nuclear forces, under discussion in 1987, but can claim no direct success. The chief cause of this is not their particular strategic or tactical weaknesses, nor their social composition, but the political intangibility of their targets. The nuclear arms race is largely the prerogative of the two superpowers; even those aspects of it which are within the control of other nation states are often carefully screened off from normal political debate – let alone control. Although, within parliamentary democracies at least, it is theoretically possible to affect decisions about military policy, it is exceptionally difficult for peace movements to sustain the momentum of forces strong enough to break through. Among political elites, the sort of consensus which existed among British political parties until 1980 is often strongly rooted. Among the wider population, nuclear politics may have no deep roots in present military participation, but they have the force of habitual attitudes often linked – however inappropriately – to the lessons of real military participation in the Second World War. Pro-nuclear elites may use their control of political and cultural institutions to reinforce these attitudes in the population.

The seemingly intractable problems of war-resistance and radical politics in the nuclear age are therefore interlinked. Anti-war or anti-nuclear-weapons movements cannot be sustained by the social contradictions of the arms race alone. Equally, radical social movements cannot progress without confronting the military realities which constitute so much of the framework of state and ideology. The interrelationship between the two can be traced back to the basic pattern of militarism, state and economy in the nuclear phase of total war, which affects all social movements.

Nuclear militarism is about more than nuclear weapons. They are the archetype of the capital-intensive weapons systems which, as Mary Kaldor's study shows, characterise contemporary militarism as a whole.[4] Highly sophisticated – according to Kaldor – 'baroque' weaponry changes the nature of the relationship between arms, economy and society. It requires a state-supported (but not necessarily state-owned) arms industry; it does not, however, require the state to support, control or still less own much of the rest of the national economy. Although the strategic reasons for the state to retain extensive direct control over many basic national industries and services may not disappear, they are greatly weakened. Large conscript armies and mass-production munitions industries are a thing of the past, as far as the most technologically advanced military powers are concerned. State intervention and the welfare state may survive for other reasons but, to the extent that they have been based on military necessity, they are likely to be threatened.

The political consequence of this is that the state cannot now be relied upon, as it could in the second phase of total war, to provide basic social needs. This implies the danger of the state cutting services which individuals and groups cannot provide for themselves. At the same time, however, it may create a great deal more involvement for society in providing for its own needs, instead of passive dependence on the state. In discussing the social implications of military participation in the Second World War, we noted the centralised and bureaucratic character of the 'military–democratic' state. Military participation implied at best a distorted form of social participation. The relative decline of centralised state bureaucracy obviously opens up dangers of restoring large areas of economic and social life to private capitalism. But it also opens up possibilities of more genuine social participation: cooperative ownership and production, workers' self-management, involvement of consumers in the running of services, etc. Such possibilities not only involve social advance: they also have political implications, since adapting state apparatuses to different forms of social organisation modifies the state. Examples of this can be seen, at least at the local state level, in Western Europe.

The 'military–democratic' state was based on a bonding of state and society, and a relative unity within the state of its military and social apparatuses. The 'nuclear' state opens up a large gap between the military branches of the state and the underlying society; but this also tends to become a divide within the state. Lesser organs, such as the local state and educational, health and welfare services, can become arenas both for expressing social needs and for opposing nuclear militarism. The social and military contradictions become, to a certain extent, conflicts within the field of the state.

Just as Britain was a strong case of the 'military–democratic' form, so it now exhibits a particularly sharp form of nuclear militarism. A society which, in living memory, was mobilised almost to the last man (and woman) is now the most thoroughly demobilised of all major states. Even the infrastructure of conscription, which remains in the US (and was activated for Vietnam), has been dismantled in the UK. Civil defence, which is a serious business in neutral states such as Switzerland, has nowhere been more thoroughly abandoned as a means of protecting citizens. (In the UK it is an ideological joke, especially since the government's 1980 propaganda disaster, *Protect and Survive*). Despite the strong attachment of sections of the political establishment to the traditional armed services, it is commitment to nuclear weapons which has long been a litmus test for both conservatism and right-wing social democracy. Little of the institutional basis of military participation survives, although the ideological residues may be more potent.

Britain has thus undergone a more radical transition in its relationship to militarism than other states. The British state, traditionally *laissez faire*, became radically interventionist as a result of the first two phases of total war. In the nuclear age it has embraced the logic of nuclearisation more fully than other states, and ultimately this has been reflected in the Thatcherite attempt to divest the state of many of its no-longer-strategic assets. British society has been profoundly affected by this transformation: the disciplined military–democratic culture of the early post-war years has been eroded by demilitarisation and affluence. Britain's clear decline, as world power, empire and economy, has provided fewer and fewer symbols with which to maintain national ideology and cohesion.

To an extent, of course, this is also true of other European countries. Only in the superpowers is there now a real basis for militaristic nationalism. In Europe (East even more than West), national pride can no longer be based on military prowess. And yet most European societies are more disciplined by proximity to the geopolitical fault in the Continent, as well as by the surviving forms of military participation. Britain stands well to the fore of the general military demobilisation, and its economic, social and political crisis has been the more acute partly in consequence of this. It is a striking confirmation of the transformation of the relationship between militarism and society that the consistently high level of British military expenditure has done virtually nothing to offset these trends.

Implications for social movements

The logic of the changing relationship between state and society is that the anti-nuclear movements must see the opening up of social contradictions as necessary for their long-term success, while social groups with interests in the welfare state must be prepared to take a stand against militarism. For anti-nuclear movements the strategic options seem to be: either to remain isolated as 'single-issue' movements, in which case the lack of real social involvement in military matters is likely to condemn them to long-term ineffectiveness; or to find a way, while maintaining their specific aims and identities, to become part of a broader social process. Theoretically, there is a third option: to campaign for an alternative form of mass military participation, but this seems wholly anachronistic. If we are right about the 'dead end' of war and strategy, then the goal of peace movements must be to continue to demilitarise society, not to define an alternative militarism. Peace movements must actually be about peace, not (primarily) defence.

The task of demilitarising society involves two main planks. One is the direct and obvious job which the peace movement has been doing, of opposing military preparations. The other, however, is to assist movements which advance social participation to reclaim for positive non-militarist purposes the social space which the limited *de facto* demilitarisation of much of nuclear society has created.

The decline of socio-economic 'participation' via the centralised welfare state has also meant the decline of the traditional, centralised labour movement. The opening of a wider social space has also seen more varied and fragmented social movements claiming it. Instead of unified trade-union movements dominated by male manual workers, we have more variegated workers' organisations in which white-collar and professional workers, and women in all occupational groups, are playing larger roles. The boom created larger ethnic minorities in all major capitalist societies: their communities are now claiming a role. Women, and sexual minority groups, no longer accept their subordination: their movements have an extraordinarily wide influence on society. The decomposition of traditional families has created new interest groups, such as single parents. The decline of cities has called forth community groups concerned with housing and urban facilities generally. The rapid advance of industrialism, often destructive of the environment, has led to the formation of ecological campaigns. And so on. A vast range of new forces represent the more varied interests of society, and demand that the state changes to meet their needs.

In confronting the state, however, social movements of all kinds meet fundamental problems. Many of these are familiar. There is the difficulty, traditionally identified by Marxists, that the state systematically favours the interests of large-scale capital. There is the problem of bureaucratisation which affects every area of state activity. There is the other main problem emphasised by Marxists, that the state exists to repress social movements: the police have been greatly expanded both in number and in the range of tasks and means of control which they adopt. But there is also, and in a sense ultimately, the problem of the military apparatus.

Traditionally, Marxists lumped together the armed forces

with the prisons and police as the repressive arms of the state. So it may have seemed in the nineteenth century, when there was much military repression of the working class but little continuous warfare. In the twentieth century, however, the military have been primarily a means of inter-state conflict and only secondarily a means of internal repression. In most advanced capitalist societies, this function has increasingly become a specialised police concern. Even such a major class conflict as the 1984-85 miners' strike in Britain was dealt with by para-militarising the police, rather than by bringing in the troops. Thus nuclear militarism is increasingly pure militarism: indeed, its technology is such that it has minimal potential for policing. Even the apartheid state in South Africa might hesitate to 'nuke' its own subject population. What we are confronted with, in the end, is an immensely powerful, expensive apparatus of unprecedented destructive capacity which exists almost entirely to service real, or hypothetical, conflicts between states.

What, it may be asked, has this sort of militarism to do with the social movements which we have been discussing? The people they seek to mobilise do not on the whole participate directly in this militarism. It is remote, abstract; it may even seem to provide a space within which social movements may act. Its potential for actual war, nuclear war, catastrophically threatens the whole of society; but how directly is this threat felt by most of society? Their connection with nuclear militarism, as a form of militarism in the here and now rather than as a threat of ultimate annihilation, needs to be established.

The problem of this militarism for social movements is deep but not always easy to grasp, for it is as much a matter of culture as one of tangible social and economic facts. Nuclear militarism represents a principle of social and state organisation which is directly opposed to the life-creating, life-expanding, democratic impulses of most basic social movements. The essence of nuclear militarism is not only its capacity for instantaneous destruction, with its distortion of all the best impulses of our culture and technology. It is a fundamentally restrictive principle of social organisation, which mentally coerces society into accepting a framework of international conflict as an overriding reality. It places at the heart of the state a huge commitment of resources to military facilities which can no longer be rationally connected to the interests of society.

The tangible effects of nuclear militarism are thus evident in the structures of the state, in militarism's privileged claims for resources. These claims have crucial social effects – the diversion of resources from social need to weaponry. But the cultural and ideological effects on society are equally real. It cannot be an accident that the period of greatest play for emancipatory impulses in our culture was from the mid-1960s through into the 1970s, when detente relaxed the Cold War and loosened its ideological hold on societies. The 'new Cold War' can be seen as a process of re-tightening, and E.P. Thompson is right to emphasise that the peace movements must be as concerned with resisting this as with removing missiles. Indeed, as he suggests, the task for the peace movement is largely one of creating cultural links which cut across the tendency of Cold War militarism to freeze peoples in nations and blocs.[5] When international culture is fractured by the Cold War, the responses of our culture as a whole are weakened.

If the values which sustain all the social movements for change suffer when nuclear militarism is in the ascendant, then all such movements must make the challenge to this militarism a central part of their projects.

Peace politics and socialism

This argument for a connection of anti-militarism and radical social movements should not be confused with the traditional reductionist argument that nuclear disarmament can only come under socialism. Nor should it be seen as implying particular tactics, for questions of practical political intervention cannot be settled at the general level on which we have been arguing. What has been suggested is that the relationship between nuclear militarism and society implies a general strategic relationship between peace movements and wider movements for social change.

This argument, far from reproducing standard socialist arguments poses radical challenges to them. These follow from the critique of historical socialist positions which has been generated throughout this book. It has been effectively argued that socialists of all kinds have underestimated militarism and war. The primacy given to socio-economic relations has rendered socialists weak in understanding the mobilising capacity of military relations, and their implications for social change. This is reflected in specific theoretical weaknesses of early Marxism, which was very much a product of mid-nineteenth century 'peace'. The decisive proof of socialism's difficulties with war is to be found in its failure to understand the way in which the processes of total war generate the conditions in which different models of socialism itself – revolutionary, reformist and Stalinist – have been realised. It has been argued that, despite the origins of socialist ideas in the contradictions of nineteenth-century capitalism, the success of the principal forms of socialist politics has depended on their practical evolution under conditions of twentieth-century total war. It can be concluded from this that both the individual positions and the debates between them (reform versus revolution, for example) are unlikely to be adequate in the changed conditions of nuclear militarism and society.

Traditional socialist politics, both revolutionary and reformist, have been marked, then, by experiences of war which they have little understood. One consequence of this is that, carried over into the nuclear age, they bring with them positions and attitudes which are historically anachronistic. This is most obviously true of attitudes to war and political violence, but it applies more generally to concepts of political action and organisation. Many of the new left and feminist critiques of traditional Marxism and social reform would be greatly strengthened if they recognised the fact that what they are criticising is, effectively, the socialism of total war. It is not just that traditional socialisms are openly militaristic in one sense or another; it is also that the forms of state and social organisation which they represent are those associated with the era of mass militarism, and are in decay with it.

Although both revolutionary and reformist traditions in the twentieth century have contained important anti-militarist strands, they have been based on the fundamental idea that war may be necessary to socialism. While socialists have protested at the horrors of modern war, they have rarely questioned the basic pragmatic approach to war generated by the nineteenth-century attitudes of Marx and Engels. A particular war, or form of warfare, may have been objected to, and the objection fused with an elementary moral condemnation. But war in general has rarely become the object of systematic socialist critique – in a number of ways an understandable situation, since there were indeed many real choices within wars before 1945. Socialists recognised the opportunities which wars presented them, if not in theory then at least in practice, and the advantages which could sometimes be achieved by a war policy.

For revolutionary socialists, it has been axiomatic that the old ruling class and state will attempt to resist their overthrow, so that revolutionaries must be prepared to arm to achieve or maintain victory. In practice, revolutionary movements have not only tended to *become* militarised, but have often adopted military forms from the outset. For reformist socialists, it has been equally axiomatic that, where there is even a minimal identification between working-class interests and a democratic state, they have a duty to support the state's wars. Although less directly militarised in themselves, reformist movements have accepted and often positively identified with the dominant militarism of the state.

From this it has followed that socialism became an overwhelmingly militarist and statist idea. Both existing 'models' of socialism have embraced the centralised, bureaucratic methods of war-mobilisation as methods of creating socialist advance. However extreme and exceptional the Russian civil war was, however much an aberration the eulogies of 'war communism' produced by later critics of Stalinism (Trotsky, Bukharin), it is the ultra-statist model then established which became the norm for revolutionary regimes. Latter-day revolutionaries may deplore this outcome and prefer the 'genuine' revolutionary alternative of socialist democracy, but they have not explained how revolutions can avoid the militarist-statist result. Similarly, however much reformist socialists recognise a problem of bureaucracy, the statist model of war mobilisation remains a key reference point for success. So long as they accept the legitimacy of the military apparatus, a key element of secretive, centralised, bureaucratic state power will remain far beyond democratic control. A politics which fails to challenge this is unlikely to move seriously beyond statism in general.

One of the major difficulties in moving beyond socialist–militarist politics is the unevenness of historical trends in war. The nuclear dead-end largely closes off military means of resolving conflicts among advanced Northern industrial states. But empirically, and in the short run, it quite obviously has no such general effect in the South. Although some regional conflicts are certainly inhibited and controlled by their close connections to superpower interests, this is not universally true. Theoretically, since the superpowers are involved in virtually every part of the globe, virtually any conflict has the potential for East–West escalation. But in practice the limits often seem clear, and wars are all too possible. Socialists in the advanced world are overly inclined to see progressive, anti-imperialist content even in inter-state wars in the Third World, while revolutionary struggles receive general support.[6] The extent to which both 'old' anti-imperialist and 'new' nuclear-age critiques of war apply to Third World wars and revolutions is often neglected.

However, many wars are actually wars of national ruling classes and budding regional imperialists. Moreover, since many advanced Third World states now possess nuclear technology, their conflicts are developing a potential for mutual destruction which replicates that of the superpowers. In the decades to come, therefore, the nuclear limit will increasingly apply to all major wars, in the Third World as much as the Northern hemisphere.

Among these wars there are still genuine national revolutionary struggles. Even liberals and Christians find it difficult to deny that faced, say, with the armed intransigence of the apartheid state, armed struggle may be justified; or that faced with the invasion of the US-backed Contras, Nicaragua may need to defend its revolution. Taken in isolation, or in the context of the uneven tendency of war to become self-defeating, this is obviously true. But it is equally important not to confuse a statement that in South Africa (or wherever) armed struggle is justifiable in principle with the argument that it is actually the best, or the most important, method of struggle available. Mass social action involves more people and is more likely to lead to some form of democratic state; armed struggle may or may not assist this. One of the elements involved here is that, despite uneven development, national politics do not develop in isolation from other countries. The values, ideologies and culture of protest are worldwide, and just as armed struggle in the Third World has an (often damaging) influence on the culture of revolt in the West, so the values of our peace movements may have an indirect influence on mass movements in South Africa and elsewhere.

While the identification of sections of the Western left with movements for change in the Third World is a sign of healthy internationalism, an over-identification with the method of armed struggle is very questionable. At the very least it suggests a vicarious attachment to methods which are overwhelmingly redundant as serious political tactics in Western countries. At worst it has led to disastrous attempts to ape armed struggle in the actions of small terrorist groups. More commonly perhaps, the domestic corollary of international guerilla struggle is a preference for aggressive modes of action and quasi-militaristic modes of organisation. Physical confrontation on the streets may be actively sought (although this is not to deny that it is also provoked by the police). Socialist organisations may borrow the structures and language of militarism. They may define themselves as 'combat organisations' locked in direct conflict with a centralised state. This justifies strict centralism, discipline and internal security, which in turn deny any prospect of democracy among their members. This was the common fate of revolutionary organisations in Western Europe after 1968.[7]

It is not only among would-be revolutionaries that the influence of military forms can be found. The official Communist Parties have long retained hierarchical command organisations, even while advocating 'pluralism' and parliamentary roads to socialism. This situation can be traced back to the militarisation of the Russian Revolution, although it also has roots in the CP's attempts to ensure the absolute loyalty of its members in the polarised politics of the inter-war, Second World War and Cold War years. Socialist parties, too, have often become parties of state power in the context of total war. The British Labour Party experienced its most authoritarian regime in the 1940s and 1950s: the discipline of war and reconstruction was extended to party organisation. This was also the period of its greatest success. It does not follow, however, that this model can be recreated today. Our analysis would suggest that a contemporary model of political organisation should have an openness to a wide range of social movements, and should reflect the libertarian and radical-democratic impulses which many of them project.

The decline of the early post-war model of the Keynesian welfare state has left political space which has been successfully occupied by 'anti-statist' forces of the right. This 'anti-statism', for example of Thatcherism or Reaganomics, is of course founded on a central contradiction. It is a very selective opposition to statism: it diminishes the economic and welfare roles of the state, while increasing its policing and military roles. (Overall, therefore, it leads to an increase, rather than a reduction, in state expenditure and real taxation levels.) On the other hand, the left has not yet developed an effective non-statist, or less statist, alternative, although some of the elements of this may exist. One reason for this is that it has not yet understood that any alternative must be based on a thoroughgoing anti-militarism. This is necessary, not only to expose the contradictions of right-wing 'anti-statism', but also to develop any real momentum for the left.

The essence of a non-statist socialism, it might be quite widely agreed, is a reliance on the democratic, cooperative efforts of groups of producers, users, consumers, etc. This emphasis is quite different from the reliance on the centralised state, or on the individual enterprise in the market advocated by the right. Such an approach does not eliminate the state (but nor does the approach of any significant political force on the right). What it does is to change the basis of the relationship between social groups and the state. Where previous socialisms were based on the state's definitions of social needs, a non-statist socialism envisages that the state creates a framework of support for social groups defining their own needs and pursuing their goals.

Such an approach could not be realised by militaristic seizure of existing state power, either through revolutionary means or by a sweeping electoral victory envisaged by classical reformists. On the contrary, it must inevitably be based on a gradual process of building democratic initiative and self-organisation in large areas of society, in tandem with a process of decentralising state power. Such an approach can be called a hegemonic strategy: attempting to build up a practical basis of support in society as a precondition for political change. The concept of 'hegemony' employed by socialists advocating this sort of approach derives from the Italian Marxist, Antonio Gramsci.[8] The images of political struggle which are present in his work are themselves of a military kind, but they have a relevance in analysing the structures of society, militarism and state power today.

Gramsci advocated a political version of trench warfare

(war of position) rather than an all-out assault on state power (war of manoeuvre). He saw state power as a repressive citadel surrounded by outer trenches and fortifications, consisting of institutions which diffused its ideological dominance in society. Writing in fascist Italy, which he saw as an 'integral state' of repressive and ideological control, he believed that only a socialist movement which struggled in the outer trenches would ever be in a position to attack political power.

Gramsci's ideas are relevant today not because, as his Eurocommunist epigones argue, they are a prescription for gradual socialist advance in a parliamentary regime; but, on the contrary, because his bleak model of the relationship of state and society has some applicability today despite parliamentary government. If our analysis is right, the repressive core of state power, and above all militarism, has become *less* accessible to any form of direct political assault. Pure, nuclear-centred militarism generates as a by-product extremely sophisticated means of defeating any insurrection. At the same time it dispenses with the politically vulnerable mass conscript armies on which revolutionary movements have historically relied. This militarism, with its extreme centralisation of power, also renders itself relatively immune to democratic political control. As C. Wright Mills argued in the 1950s (and the analysis was largely correct even if his theoretical model can be questioned), nuclear militarism generates a small 'power elite' of top political, military and business leaders who control the key issues of war and peace.[9] The normal processes of the party system hardly touch these issues, partly because a consensus has been constructed to defend this concentration of political–military power.

The activities of peace movements in the 1980s have amounted to a direct assault on the centres of power in nuclear militarism. They have had tremendous success in exposing the very existence of this power, and in stimulating debate on suppressed issues. They have also exposed the weakness of the social underpinning for nuclear weaponry, forcing political elites on to the defensive especially over new weapons systems. They have not, however, fundamentally shaken the centres of nuclear power. A more deeply based hegemonic social movement is necessary for this.

This is not to write off the peace movements: they have achieved more than anyone could have imagined possible just a few years ago. They may yet, in alliance with particular political forces, change the military policies of a number of states, and so contribute to a process of disarmament and detente. They have made a unique contribution to opening up international political and cultural space on the left, within Western Europe, across the East–West divide, and to some extent globally. The peace movements have, moreover, been a major focus of radical mobilisation in response to a general rightward drift in Western societies. But their longer-term impact may depend on a broader-based reversal of this rightward tendency, across a number of societies. They need to be part of a wider advance of social movements which can democratise society, give society greater control over the state, and bring to political power parties which are committed to this process. Only then are we likely to see a sustained effort to undermine nuclear militarism which has a real chance of success.

The problem, both for the peace movement and the left, is quite simply that the main historical precedents for such radical popular movements are war situations. Radical social movements have generally come in the train of war mobilisation: the success of both revolution and reform has owed an enormous amount to this. We have to develop a social and political movement on a different basis. This is an opportunity as well as a problem because, for the first time, radical movements can develop without carrying with them particular forms of militarism which distort or even defeat their social goals. Both revolutionary militarism and democratic militarism have had their day, at least in the advanced industrial world.

The problem is to identify situations other than war situations which will stimulate social majorities actively seeking change; and to find agencies other than the centralised state which can lead and organise them. Of course we are not simply trying to identify a different sort of crisis which can lead to the kind of seizure of power by socialist forces that has previously occurred in war conditions. As we have already seen, the process of change may be different. There is therefore no point in reinstating catastrophic economic crisis, beloved of the more traditional schools of Marxism, as the locus of change. Economic catastrophes in themselves, as the interwar slump and, more recently, the onset of generalised recession in the 1970s have shown, do not produce radical change. They are more likely to result in forms of reaction. We need, indeed, a more complex, layered, conception of the accumulation of crises which shows how economy, society, culture and politics interact – and how they create the conditions in which change may develop.

The most relevant general conceptions of crisis are those which derive, again, from the work of Gramsci. His idea of 'organic crisis' – a crisis of social relations, culture and ideology as well as of economics and state power – has been fruitfully applied by Stuart Hall to contemporary British conditions. Just as Gramsci argued that the organic crisis of early twentieth-century Italian society produced the 'integral' repression and ideology of fascism, Hall sees the specific decline of post-war Britain as stimulating the growth of 'authoritarian populism'.[10] While the main focus of this was originally identified as the drive towards 'law and order',[11] the Falklands war was seen as bringing out crucial dimensions of nationalism and patriotism.[12] The 'crisis' of British society is one which encompasses the world role of the national economy and state as well as its social organisation and culture.

Such a concept of crisis is nationally formulated, and could not be applied directly to any other society. This is a difficulty, however, only for those theories – such as many classical Marxist approaches – which start from general concepts of capitalism and fail to recognise that politics and society remain largely national. An approach such as that advocated here, while trying to discuss general trends in the relationship of war and society, must always recognise that modern wars are fought between nation-states. National societies therefore have individual experiences both of war and political development. We have emphasised the uniqueness of both 'models' that we have discussed: the Russian Revolution and British social democracy. The development of political alternatives can only be discussed really concretely in a national context, although there are broad international currents at work.

The most important of these is clearly Green politics. The Green movement originated in West Germany as a successor to the extra-parliamentary opposition and an expression of the environmental and anti-nuclear-power battles of the 1970s. It became a national political force as a result of the peace movement of the early 1980s. It has developed into a significant radical presence in a number of European countries, largely as a result of the international nature of the peace movement. As a minority party, Greens clearly confront all sorts of practical problems which may make their independent political existence precarious: in Germany, the problems of coalition which follow from electoral success; in Britain, the difficulty of breaking through electorally at all. (Nevertheless, independent Green parties have been more successful in building themselves up than their revolutionary socialist forerunners which grew out of the radical movements of the 1960s.)

More important than specific party developments, however, is the fact that Green ideas have given a general political coherence to the individual causes (nuclear weapons, nuclear power, the environment, anti-racism, feminism, etc.) around which people have become active. This coherence is relevant to activists within mainstream left-wing parties as well as to those who form the new Green parties. Green ideas generally contain their own version of an 'organic crisis', which includes nature as well as culture, society and state. The future certainly lies in bringing together these ideas with the understanding of economic realities which has been at the heart of socialist ideas.

Anti-militarism has been axiomatic to the Green movement, and in this sense the rethinking of war which is proposed in this book is a contribution to the development of ideas for a new Green left. At the centre of Green and peace movement practice in the 1980s have been the problems of defence policy; and it is our relationship with these that we now turn.

The politics of defence

We have stressed that the most active phase of Cold War ideology corresponded to the period of transition from the mass militarism of the Second World War to the nuclear-dominated militarism of the late 1950s onwards. After the early challenge to nuclear weapons (especially in Britain), the nuclear arms race was accompanied by a period of relative ideological demobilisation during which a wide range of social movements emerged. Only when new peace movements developed in the early 1980s – essentially out of the social movements of the 1960s and 1970s – was Cold War ideology reactivated in Europe. Indeed, only when challenged did political leaders find it necessary to justify to a mass audience the rapid expansion of weaponry which had proceeded throughout the 1970s. The responses of national leaders varied, of course, according to the geopolitical fractures which had appeared in the once-monolithic Cold War blocs. There was a world of difference between the evangelical anti-communism of the American New Right and the cautious strategic formulations of many Western European governments. The British Tories drew on an ideology of 'the Soviet threat' which, while falling well short of US excesses, was remarkably crude by comparison with most Western European arguments.

The nuclear disarmament movements which emerged so rapidly, and thus initially possessed an ideological advantage over most governments, saw themselves as peace movements. They were defined by their opposition to nuclear weaponry, rather than by their support for any alternative military positions. Implicitly, if not in formal policy, they were thoroughgoing anti-military movements. Only as governments and pro-nuclear political forces recovered from the initial shock of the peace movements, and began a political counter-offensive, were peace movements forced to confront difficult issues about which military alternatives they favoured. The fact that the peace movements affected major political forces quite quickly – notably opposition social-democratic parties – increased this pressure, since mainstream political parties certainly could not reduce their nuclear commitments without clarifying their 'defence' stance.

Many parties which were affected by the peace movements did not, of course, reject all nuclear weapons: the British Labour Party was altered more radically than most continental socialist parties. It moved from the 1979 Labour government's all-round pro-nuclear stance to a 1981 support for full unilateral nuclear disarmament. Those in the peace movements who recognised the importance of such shifts could not but be aware that they might at the same time cause difficulties in getting anti-nuclear parties elected. Labour's movement to unilateralism accelerated the splitting off of the pro-nuclear Social Democrats, which was obviously likely to weaken Labour's chances. Despite the mass support for peace movements, it was not always clear that even partial anti-nuclear positions, such as those widely adopted on the Continent, would prove electorally successful. Public opinion polls, which recorded consistent majorities against the new cruise and Pershing missiles (even in Britain), showed in most cases equally consistent support for maintaining existing nuclear weapons and for NATO as an alliance.

Many in the peace movements have therefore felt it necessary to develop 'alternative defence policies', both to enhance the credibility of their opposition to particular nuclear systems, and to offer a framework around which policies for sympathetic political parties might be formulated. Such policies are not acceptable to all sections of the peace movement: they are objected to by both traditional pacifists and revolutionary Marxists, who believe it is inappropriate to suggest alternative ways of defending 'capitalist' states. It is important to look at the problems involved in the light of the perspective outlined in this book.

It is not the principle of 'defence', in the abstract, which should be questioned. Even more than in the Second World War, the vast majority of society have an interest in the existing social arrangements and state. The mass of the working class and the middle class benefit from and identify with existing political arrangements; many even have a small property stake, if only in their own houses. (A major part of the activity of the labour movement, and even of socialists, is the 'defence' of the state as it developed from the Second World War – against right-wing governments!) So there should be no problem, in principle, in supporting the military defence of Western parliamentary democracies against external threats: providing that such threats can be shown to exist, and that relevant (and not self-defeating) military means are available. It is here, of course, that the problems of any meaningful defence strategy arise.

It is not, moreover, the existence of a Soviet military threat to Western Europe which is in doubt. Versions of targetting plans have been published, so that people in British cities can have some idea of the missiles directed against them. No peace campaigners who have distributed leaflets showing the effect of a bomb on their locality could deny the reality of this Soviet threat. What can be denied is, first, that this threat is any more than the symmetrical counterpart to the Western threat to Soviet and East European peoples; and, second, that there is any genuine defence against it.

Western strategic experts generally accept that there is no serious evidence of any Soviet intention, plan or interest in a military invasion of Western Europe. Unlike Nazi Germany, the Soviet Union is not aggressively expansionist in that sense, however much it would like to extend its political influence and economic access to the West. The Soviet Union keeps large land forces in Eastern Europe, partly to maintain its control there. The use of these forces against Western Europe can be envisaged if East–West issues, more likely military or political than territorial, unsettle relations to the point where the USSR sees war as likely and decides to act first. Alternatively, and more probably, this could occur if a regional war in the Third World destabilises East–West relations to the point where a general war seems likely.

In either case, it is the general pattern of East–West rivalry, rather than any specific Soviet intention or interest in conquering Western Europe, which is more likely to produce an attack. Moreover, since that is the case, there would be little reason for such a war to be limited to the conventional conquest of particular European countries and resistance to that. Both superpowers and alliances are likely to see their interests as a whole as being involved; escalation of the war beyond conventional battle is highly probable. Even if the war was begun conventionally, it is likely to become nuclear (at least at the battlefield level) quite quickly. By the time it has involved attacks on Britain, some way from the East–West border, it is almost certain to have become nuclear. Indeed, since it would be obvious that any war was likely to become a major war, there would be a considerable incentive for a pre-emptive nuclear first strike which would invalidate all preparations for conventional defence. Escalation could indeed prove instantaneous.

In this context, some 'alternatives' to nuclear weapons are clearly as or more dangerous than nuclear weapons themselves. 'Strong conventional defence', if it means that NATO acquires stronger offensive conventional capacities, or even a greater capacity for sustained conventional resistance, is extremely risky. On the one hand, it could enable political and military commanders to believe that it is possible to have a conventional war in Europe without nuclear escalation, so making war more likely. But any war in central Europe, however 'limited', would be catastrophic for tens of millions of people. On the other hand, the belief that there was 'space' for a conventional war could mean that a 'limited' conventional conflict would be allowed to develop into an extremely wide and destructive conventional war. Such a war would not only involve an appalling number of casualties in itself: since escalation is a law of war, it would involve the risk that nuclear weapons would be used. Even if battlefield nuclear weapons had been withdrawn from central Europe; even, indeed, if all nuclear weapons had been withdrawn from the entire continent; or even – to take the limiting case – if the superpowers themselves had undertaken nuclear disarmament: in all these cases, an all-out conventional war could and probably would still escalate into a nuclear conflict. Nuclear weapons, as is repeatedly argued by their proponents, cannot be uninvented. The conclusion to be drawn from this truism is not, however, that we must permanently maintain and develop our nuclear arsenals. It is, much more radically, that no war should ever be contemplated between states which are nuclear-capable.

The case for 'strong conventional defence' comes from two main directions: from the generals (such as successive NATO Commanders in Europe), for whom it is a partial alternative within the context of a general nuclear defence; and from politicians (such as the leaders of the British Labour Party), for whom it is a general alternative to nuclear weapons. The motives of the two groups may be quite different, but their policies are likely to converge in practice if significant nuclear arms reductions change the military and political context.

In the context of a powerful political process of detente and disarmament, therefore, 'strong conventional defence' could just about represent an important stepping stone away from the nuclear arms race. Considered as a defence policy in its own right, however, it is a nonsense. It only exemplifies the dangers of military strategy in the nuclear age, possibly to a greater degree than a nuclear 'defence'. At least with nuclear weapons, strategists and politicians make strong distinctions between possession and use – even if these could much too

easily break down. The defensive quality of nuclear weapons is widely held to lie in their deterrent value, not in their physical use which many agree would be self-defeating. Of course, as we have seen, the central contradiction of 'deterrence' is that it is only viable if use is conceivable. This has led to attempts to refine nuclear weaponry, to make its use more plausible, so that battlefield nuclear weapons are in a sense more dangerous than strategic weapons, because their use can be more easily envisaged.

For precisely the same reasons that battlefield nuclear weapons are such a dangerous concept, 'strong conventional defence' is exceptionally risky. No one has even tried to make a clear-cut distinction between deterrence and use in such a strategy. All the evidence is that generals and politicians believe – without much of the equivocation that affects nuclear strategy – that strong conventional forces could and would be used. If they were, it would quickly be demonstrated that, far from genuinely defending the people of Europe, they would lead to a suicidal and genocidal war. At the very least, millions of Germans would die; with any escalation, the danger of all-out nuclear extermination would not be far away.

The simple truth is that total military defence of any kind, conventional as well as nuclear, is impossible in any sense that is free from utterly unacceptable risks for the people of Europe and the world. This may be difficult to understand, in a world that is still living on the myths of a world war for 'freedom' and 'democracy'. Politically and intellectually, peoples as well as states are still conditioned by past experience of war. In the case of the United States and Britain, this experience was far removed from the worst episodes of the 1939-45 period. But even the Russians, Poles, Germans, Japanese and Chinese, who saw far more of the horror of that war, would have to make huge imaginative leaps to grasp the absolutely greater horrors of nuclear war. The awareness which exists does not yet sufficiently inform the policies of any major state.

However valid politically, as we have suggested, the very

concept of 'defence' is therefore extremely problematic in a military sense. Purely defensive wars are rare enough in history, and highly unlikely in the nuclear age. Defence and offence go together, and in the nuclear age produce a threat of mutual annihilation. While the other side's nuclear weapons are indeed threatening, so are 'ours', for they invite the potential enemy to target us with their missiles. The defence which people require in the nuclear age is defence against war as such: against the whole system of international relations, strategy and war-preparation which may produce war. The most important defence is not, therefore, military at all, but political. This is not playing with words, but a simple recognition of the irresolvable contradictions of *any* military strategy on the part of states or alliances which have entered the age of nuclear warfare. Military defence of peoples and societies as a whole is simply not possible with a reasonable degree of confidence that appalling risks can be avoided.

The politics of nuclear disarmament, detente and international cooperation are the only safe basis for defence. The main task for the peace movements is not, therefore, to propose alternative ways either of fighting wars or of maintaining deterrence. It is rather to find ways of undermining the arms race, developing cultural and political relationships between people and movements across the Cold War divide, and pushing governments into constructive measures of both disarmament and political change – within and between blocs.[13]

Any discussion of 'defence policies' is only meaningful within this context. The main reason that the peace movement is forced into an engagement with non-nuclear military defence is that it has to start at the point of awareness of the public at large, and to a lesser extent parties and governments, if it is to have any chance of influencing events. As has already been suggested, peoples as well as governments are still thinking about war in ways which reflect the past rather than present prospects. The assumption that military defence is possible has hardly been questioned either by public or by politicians, although the whole argument for deterrence contains an implicit recognition that in reality it is very difficult to envisage conditions in which a war might rationally be fought. Politicians advocating nuclear disarmament often seem to regard it as their first task to assure the public not only that they will be defended, but that all possible non-nuclear means will be deployed.

Peace movements should be more honest and put forward the case that there is *no* real military defence in the nuclear age. If we align ourselves tactically with the advocates of 'strong conventional defence', it must not be in order to foster illusions that such a prospect is safely available, but because any form of nuclear disarmament can be used as a constructive step towards wider disengagement. If we put forward 'alternative defence policies' ourselves, these should be of a sort which clearly point in the direction of political change rather than alternative forms of warfare. Interestingly, in this context, proposals have recently been revived for a form of 'citizen's territorial defence' along the lines advocated by some left-wingers in Britain in 1939-45.[14] While in one sense this seems like a constructive proposal, since it breaks down the professionalisation of the armed forces and relies on limited weaponry, it is also fundamentally anachronistic. It proposes to revive mass participation in military defence at a time when such defence is increasingly impossible and when society as a whole has largely moved beyond military involvement. Such proposals would reinforce the illusion that the next war may be similar to the last, which is one of the biggest obstacles to a breakthrough in opposition to nuclear militarism. It would, in a sense, remilitarise society, when the peace movement has the opportunity to turn a large measure of *de facto* demilitarisation into a more positive commitment to peace.

A more relevant concept is that of 'non-provocative defence' argued by a number of European writers. It is proposed that West European countries should adopt weaponry, force levels and deployments of such a kind as would clearly indicate to the Soviet Union the lack of any offensive capability or intention.[15] The aim, instead, would be to develop anti-weapon systems which would indicate a willingness to resist territorial incursions, without responding by offensive attacks. Such a stance would promise to impose considerable costs on an invader, but without threatening all-out war. It would represent a recognition that war of the kind pursued in 1939-45, let alone that envisaged by current strategists, is no longer feasible. But, by promising some military resistance, which could be reinforced by unarmed popular opposition, it could make a contribution to answering popular anxieties about 'leaving us defenceless' as well as posing genuine problems for a state which was considering any sort of military incursion.

While such a strategy has some plausibility, its advocacy has major problems. Although there is a clear enough distinction in principle between 'non-provocative defence' and what we have called 'strong conventional defence', it may be hard to make this distinction clear in political debate. In a context of enormous nuclear over-armament, where 'strong conventional defence' (with or without nuclear weapons) is on offer from major military and political forces, any argument for a conventional military strategy may appear as an echo of this policy. At the very least, any alternative defence policy which the peace movements (or political forces close to them) argue for should be clearly subordinate to a political strategy. 'Non-provocative defence' is only a partial military defence against partial military aggression; there can be no total military defence against the total attack of which nuclear-armed states are capable. The central thrust of any anti-nuclear politics should be that the only defence for any society in the nuclear age is political rather than military. Military attack must be prevented, not fought off; war must be permanently eliminated, not rehabilitated in 'less destructive' forms. Defence must be based, first, on establishing the political framework for regulating conflicts without war; and, second, on reversing the escalation of the arms race, so dangerous in itself, by systematic reductions in armaments.

A philosophy of 'historical pacifism'

Those who claim to hold 'philosophies' of war and peace very often ground them in some variety of religious or ethical belief. They are more likely to have an absolute objection to war itself than a historical or political approach to the changing forms of war. Indeed, within peace movements there are often considerable tensions between those who hold a philosophical position against war as such and those who are primarily interested in political measures against particular forms of militarism.

The one major philosophy which is founded on a historical conception, Marxism, is one which is associated with a pragmatic approach to war. Neither support for, nor opposition to, war in general can be a principle for Marxism. Historical materialism determines that the means of violence should be understood, and judged, within the context of the economic, social and political relations in which they are produced and used. At its most simple, this position boils down to the argument that weapons are neither good nor bad in their own right: it depends in whose hands they are. The inadequacy of this approach can be seen in the disreputable indirect apologies for Soviet nuclear weapons sometimes made by Stalinists and Trotskyists within the peace movements.

In this book we have made fundamental criticisms of the theoretical conceptions and historical interpretations of classical Marxism. With the benefit of late twentieth-century hindsight, we have tried to pinpoint the dominant role of the processes of war. Forces which were largely implicit when Marx wrote have since become powerfully explicit in world history. It is in the spirit, if not the letter, of Marx's approach to revise historical materialism by allowing fuller scope to the relations of war. In this sense, while there is little point in continuing to claim the label 'Marxist', we nevertheless need to maintain the goal – to which non-Marxist social theorists have also contributed – of a historically informed politics and social practice. This book can be seen as a contribution to a broadly-based radical and Green critique of Marxism.

Underlying the politics of war which we have been discussing there should, then, be a historical understanding of the present phase of warfare. In a basic sense, of course, there is wide recognition that nuclear weapons alter all the rules for war and peace. Very many people who supported, indeed fought in, wars before 1945 have recognised that nuclear war is utterly inconceivable. Even the strategists, politicians and military leaders with responsibility for nuclear weapons have had, as we have seen, to acknowledge this tacitly. For many, there is the clearest possible divide, and those who perceive it sometimes call themselves 'nuclear pacifists' to convey that their refusal of nuclear weapons is as absolute as the total pacifist's rejection of war itself. E.P. Thompson, for example, has described himself in these terms.[16]

The difficulty with a simple nuclear pacifism is that it suggests that the problem is a particular sort of weaponry, and tries to draw a sharp line between nuclear and non-nuclear war which cannot really be made. Just as nuclear weapons developed the potential for mass killing of civilians already present in aerial bombing, so nuclear technology has been applied to all shapes and sizes of weaponry. If lines must be drawn, a more relevant one than that between nuclear and non-nuclear weapons, or forms of warfare, is that between war involving nuclear-capable states and war which is clearly limited to non-nuclear states. But all such distinctions are relative: nuclear weapons have so altered the prospects of war that the problem can increasingly be seen to be war itself.

This is why 'historical pacifism' is better than nuclear pacifism. Nuclear pacifism tries to draw one particular line within modern warfare; historical pacifism is the belief that the problem is modern warfare in general. Nuclear pacifism is absolute but limited; historical pacifism is more conditional, but more comprehensive. Historical pacifism can be defined as the belief that war is becoming, and to a large extent has already become, redundant as a means of achieving justifiable human ends. Historical pacifism will lead us to refuse not just nuclear war, and direct preparations for it, but any war or war-preparation, however conventional, which could lead to nuclear war. Historical pacifism will lead us to ask, even of warfare which seems wholly non-nuclear, whether the mass killing involved can seriously be justified by the political goals or state interests which it purports to further. Historical pacifism will enable us to learn the lessons of past warfare, and ask of any war whether the means involved will not defeat or distort the ostensible aims.

The idea of historical pacifism advanced here would allow very much more limited scope for legitimate military activity than the concept of nuclear pacifism. Indeed, it involves reversing the basis of the argument about war and peace. Where nuclear pacifism rests on an assumption of the general legitimacy of war, and makes a case that nuclear war is exceptional and illegitimate, historical pacifism poses things the other way round. It argues that the whole historical development of warfare, of which nuclear weapons are the culmination, has undermined the assumption of the legitimacy of war. In the nuclear age, war is becoming outmoded; it is the warfare which is still justified which has to be explained.

This seems a much better way round of posing matters. Given all that we know of the murderous, genocidal and ultimately exterminist dangers of modern warfare, it is right to ask of anyone who proposes the use of military force whether this can possibly be legitimate. We need to ask – whether it is a case of the Falklands Task Force or a PLO attack on Israel, or whatever – not only whether the political goals are legitimate in themselves, but whether there is any other means of furthering them, and whether the means proposed will really achieve what is intended without causing new problems which will outweigh any positive results. We need to ask all states, and non-state organisations, which maintain military forces and use them whether their policies and actions are contributing to the overriding goal of eliminating the danger of exterminist war. This approach gives us, I hope, a standpoint for action which is relevant to the character of our age and the overriding danger which war now poses to human society.

Notes and References

Preface

1. E.P. Thompson, 'Notes on Exterminism: the last stage of civilisation', in Thompson et al., *Exterminism and Cold War*, London, Verso, 1982.
2. Anthony Giddens, *The Nation-State and Violence*, Cambridge, Polity, 1985, p. 326.

1

1. To paraphrase Marx's First Thesis on Feuerbach, the defect of most social theory of war and militarism is that it has sought to reduce war to rational, material interests: it has not considered war as practice, i.e. what people actually *do* in war. Hence again 'the active side has been developed abstractly' – in this case by military theory.
2. See the classical argument of Margaret Mead, 'Warfare is only an Invention – Not a Biological Necessity', in Leon Bramson & George W. Goethals (eds.), *War: Studies from Psychology, Sociology, Anthropology*, London, Basic Books, 1964. For a more recent discussion see David Riches, 'Violence, Peace and War in "Early" Human Society: The Case of the Eskimo', in Colin Creighton & Martin Shaw, (eds.), *The Sociology of War and Peace*, London, Macmillan, 1987.
3. For a finely argued case which nevertheless stands as an illustration of the limits of thinking on war-limitation, see Ian Clark, *Limited Nuclear War*, Oxford, Martin Robertson, 1982.
4. See the classic discussion of Raymond Aron, *War and Industrial Society*, London, OUP, 1958. For a more recent commentary, Michael Mann, 'Capitalism and Militarism', in M. Shaw (ed.), *War, State and Society*, London, Macmillan, 1984, pp. 25-46.
5. Alvin Gouldner surveyed 25 introductory textbooks published between 1945 and 1954, and found that only 275 out of a total of 17,000 pages dealt with some aspect of the causes and effects of war ('Introduction to Durkheim', *Socialism and Saint-Simon*, London, Collier-Macmillan, 1962, p. 10). A similar survey today could only show the persistence or exacerbation of relative neglect.
6. See my discussion in 'War, Imperialism and the State System: A Critique of

Orthodox Marxism for the 1980s', in M. Shaw (ed.), *War, State and Society*, pp. 47-70.

7.   See, for example, the critique of Weber in Herbert Marcuse, 'Industrialisation and Capitalism', *New Left Review* 30, March-April 1965, pp.3-17.

8.   Michael Howard, *Clausewitz*, Oxford University Press, 1984, Ch. 3. Howard interestingly stresses the ambiguity of Clausewitz's key term 'Die Schlacht'.

9.   Clausewitz, *On War*, quoted in Howard, *Clausewitz*, p.49. Emphasis added.

10. Clausewitz, *On War*, quoted in Howard, *Clausewitz*, p.70.

11. Howard, *Clausewitz*, p.70.

12. As already indicated, something of the irresolvability of this problem can be seen from Clark, *Limited Nuclear War*.

13. This idea is consciously adopted from guerrilla warfare as a general principle of strategy in a recent academic discussion: Alexander Atkinson, *Social Order and the General Theory of Strategy*, London, Routledge and Kegan Paul, 1981, p. 29.

14. See the survey of anthropological evidence and argument in Henry J.M. Claessen and Peter Skalnik, 'The Early State: Theories and Hypotheses', in Claessen & Skalnik (eds.), *The Early State*, The Hague, Mouton, 1978.

15. Or so it has been argued, not only by the Marxist Karl Kautsky, *The Origins of Christianity* (1908), London, Orbach & Chambers, 1972, esp. pp. 47-85, but also in a fascinating essay of Max Weber, 'The Social Causes of the Decay of Ancient Civilisation' (1896), in J.E.T. Eldridge (ed.), *Max Weber*, London, Nelson, 1971, pp. 254-75.

16. Mann, 'Capitalism and Militarism'.

17. For an extension of these arguments, see my 'Marxism, the State and Politics', in *Marxist Sociology Revisited*, London, Macmillan, 1985, pp. 246-68.

18. Mary Kaldor, 'Capitalism and Warfare', in E.P. Thompson, *et al.*, *Exterminism and Cold War*, London, Verso, 1982, pp. 272, 283.

19. Ibid, pp. 284-5.

2

1.   Mann, 'Capitalism and Militarism', pp. 28-9.

2.   E.P. Thompson, 'Notes on Exterminism, the Last Stage of Civilisation', in Thompson, *et al.*, *Exterminism and Cold War*.

3.   Ralph Miliband, *The State in Capitalist Society*, London, Weidenfeld and Nicolson, 1969; Nicos Poulantzas, *Political Power and Social Classes*, London, NLB, 1973; John Holloway and Sol Picciotto (eds.), *State and Capital*, London, E. Arnold, 1978.

4.   Theda Skocpol, *States and Social Revolutions*, Cambridge University Press, 1979; Peter B. Evans, Dietrich Rueschemeyer and Theda Skocpol (eds.), *Bringing the State Back In*, Cambridge University Press, 1985.

5.   Anthony Giddens, *The Nation-State and Violence*, Oxford, Polity, 1985; Ralph
      Miliband, *Class Power and State Power*, London, Verso, 1983, pp. 72-3.
6.   John Hall, 'War and the Rise of the West', in Creighton & Shaw (eds.), *The
      Sociology of War and Peace*; W.H. McNeill, *The Pursuit of Power: Technology,
      Armed Force and Society since A.D. 1000*, Oxford, Blackwell, 1983, pp. 211-212.
7.   Geoffrey Best, *War and Society in Revolutionary Europe 1770-1870*, London,
      Fontana, 1982, p.86.
8.   Ibid., p.57.
9.   Ibid.
10.   McNeill, *The Pursuit of Power*, p.242.
11.   Ibid., p.273n.
12.   Ibid., p.280.
13.   Ibid., p.292.
14.   Ibid., p.293.
15.   Friedrich Engels, 'The Force Theory' in Bernard Semmel, (ed.), *Marxism
      and the Science of War*, Oxford University Press, 1981, p.57.
16.   Brian Bond, *War and Society in Europe, 1870-1970*, London, Fontana, 1984,
      p.107.
17.   W.K. Hancock and M.M. Gowing, *British War Economy*, London, HMSO,
      1949, p.29.
18.   Ibid., pp. 20, 25.
19.   See Philip Abrams, 'The Failure of Social Reform, 1918-1920', *Past and
      Present*, 24, 1963, although for a different emphasis, Arthur Marwick, *War
      and Social Change in the Twentieth Century*, London, Macmillan, 1977.
20.   James Burnham, *The Managerial Revolution*, Harmondsworth, Penguin,
      1942.
21.   Hancock and Gowing, *British War Economy*, p.69.
22.   Ibid., p.70.
23.   Alan S. Milward, *The German Economy at War*, London, Athlone Press, 1965,
      p. 8.
24.   Ibid., p.6.
25.   Ibid., p.106.
26.   For contrasting views, see Michael Cox, 'Western Capitalism and the Cold
      War System', in Shaw (ed.), *War, State and Society*, and Fred Halliday, *The
      Making of the Second Cold War*, London, Verso, 1983.
27.   C. Wright Mills, *The Power Elite*, Oxford University Press, 1956. Although
      subsequently scorned by Marxist-influenced sociology in favour of a 'ruling
      class' theory of power, Mills' book has the virtue of a critically important,
      historically specific argument about the changing nature of power in mid-
      20th century America.
28.   E.P.Thompson, *Exterminism*, p.22.
29.   See especially Michael Kidron, *Western Capitalism since the War*, London,
      Weidenfeld & Nicolson, 1968.

30. David Holloway, *The Soviet Union and the Arms Race*, London, Yale University Press, 1983.

31. Mary Kaldor, *The Baroque Arsenal*, London, Deutsch, 1982.

32. See J.R. Camilleri, *The State and Nuclear Power: Conflict and Control in the Western World*, Brighton, Wheatsheaf, 1984.

33. This trend is apparent in the longitudinal data in Table 2, 'State Expenditure in the UK, 1910-73', in Ian Gough, 'State Expenditure in Advanced Capitalism', *New Left Review*, 92, July-August 1975. We can extract the following figures for per cent of GNP in each year:

	1910	1937	1951	1961
'Total social services'	4.2	10.9	16.1	17.6
'Military and external'	3.5	5.0	10.8	7.6

1951 was a peak year for military spending because of the Korean war (although 1910 and 1937 were also years of military build-up).

34. When Gough's figures are extended to 1971 and 1973 we find a surge in social service spending (to 23.8 and 24.9% of GNP) and a decline in military/external spending (to 6.6 and 6.4%). In an international comparison, Gough found growth rates for military spending lower than growth rates in GNP, and growth rates for civilian state spending higher than growth rates in GNP, in the period 1955-69. (Table 1, Ibid.).

35. Philip Armstrong, Andrew Glyn, John Harrison, *Capitalism Since World War II*, London, Fontana, 1984. The Reagan/Thatcher increases in military expenditure are even described as 'an aberration from their programmes for economic restoration' (p. 423).

36. The estimated increase in defence spending from 1979 to 1986 is 29.8% (public expenditure plans quoted in the *Guardian*, 16 January 1986).

37. Despite the increase in military spending just referred to, UK defence employment fell by 7% between 1979 and 1985. Peter Southwood, 'The UK Defence Industry', *Bradford Peace Research Report*, no. 8, 1985, gives the following figures (Tables 3 & 4, pp. 20 & 24):

(thousands)	1979	1985
Service Personnel	315	325.5 (est.)
Civilian staff (MoD)	247.7	174.7 (est.)
Direct employment (MoD work)	319	315
Indirect " " "	263	250
TOTAL	1144.7	1065.2

38. Michael Mann, 'The Roots and Contradictions of Modern Militarism', *New Left Review*, 162, March–April 1987.

3

1. Theda Skocpol, *States and Social Revolutions*, p.186.
2. Ibid., pp. 60-3.
3. Ibid., p. 185.
4. Richard Cobb, quoted ibid, p. 199.
5. Engels, 'The Force Theory', pp. 53-4. Emphasis in original.
6. Ibid., p. 54. Emphasis in original.
7. Karl Liebknecht, *Militarism and Anti-Militarism*, New York, Dover, 1972, p. 41.
8. The compilation of Semmel, *Marxism and the Science of War*, emphasises this Marxist tradition, at the expense of the anti-militarist politics of pre-1917 revolutionary Marxism.
9. An earlier, and in some respects a fuller version of the argument in this section is to be found in *Socialism and Militarism*, Spokesman pamphlet 74, 1981.
10. Gloden Dallas and Douglas Gill, *The Unknown Army*, London, Verso, 1985, argue that although the soldiers' revolts which they chronicle were contemporaneous with extensive workers' militancy, there was no real connection between the two.
11. Rosa Luxemburg, quoted in Norman Geras, *The Legacy of Rosa Luxemburg*, London, New Left Books, 1976, pp. 165-6.
12. Isaac Deutscher, *The Prophet Armed: Trotsky 1879-1921*, New York, Vintage nd, p. 406.
13. Ibid., pp. 469-70.
14. V.L. Lenin, *The State and Revolution*, Moscow, Progress Publishers, 1965, p. 5; Geras, *Rosa Luxemburg*.
15. Even an anti-Soviet historian such as Robert Conquest, *The Great Terror*, Harmondsworth, Penguin, 1971, recognises a fundamental shift in the character and scale of dictatorship and repression from the 1920s to the full horrors of Stalin's rule in the 1930s and 1940s.
16. Paul M. Sweezy, *The Theory of Capitalist Development*, London, Monthly Review Press, 1968, p. 346.
17. David Calleo, *The German Problem Reconsidered*, Cambridge University Press, 1978, quoted in Sarah Gordon, *Hitler, Germans and the 'Jewish Question'*, Princeton University Press, 1984, p. 100.
18. Nikolai Bukharin, *The Politics and Economics of the Transformation Period*, (ed. K.J. Tarbuck), London, Routledge and Kegan Paul, 1979.
19. See for example, E.P. Thompson, 'The Liberation of Perugia', in *The Heavy Dancers*, London, Merlin, 1985.
20. For a comparative study see Goran Therborn, 'The Rule of Capital and the Rise of Democracy', *New Left Review*, 103, May-June 1977.

21. Skocpol, *States and Social Revolutions*, p. 262.
22. Ibid., p. 257.

4

1. Mann, 'The Roots and Contradictions of Modern Militarism'. In a recent study, however, Mann has gone beyond this position (paper given to the British Sociological Association study group on the Sociology of War and Peace, Leicester, Jan. 1986).
2. Marwick, *War and Social Change in the Twentieth Century*.
3. McNeill, *The Pursuit of Power*; Maurice Pearton, *The Knowledgeable State*, London, Burnett, 1982.
4. Stanislav Andreski, *Military Organisation and Society*, 2nd edn, Berkeley/Los Angeles, University of California Press, 1971.
5. Marwick, *Britain in the Century of Total War*, Harmondsworth, Penguin, 1968.
6. Mann, 'The Roots and Contradictions of Modern Militarism'.
7. Ibid.
8. C. Wright Mills, *The Power Elite*, Oxford University Press, 1956.
9. Malcolm Chalmers, *Paying for Defence*, London, Pluto, 1985.
10. Stuart Hall, 'Authoritarian Populism: A Reply', *New Left Review*, 151, May-June 1985, p. 123.
11. Angus Calder, *The People's War*, London, Cape, 1969; Paul Addison, *The Road to 1945*, London, Cape, 1975; Marwick, *Britain in the Century of Total War*.
12. See for example Keith Middlemas, *Politics in Industrial Society*, London, Deutsch, 1979; David Coates, *The Context of British Politics*, London, Hutchinson, 1984; Colin Leys, *Politics in Britain*, London, Heinemann, 1983; G. McLennan, D. Held and S. Hall, *State and Society in Contemporary Britain*, Cambridge, Polity, 1984.
13. Kenneth O. Morgan, *Labour in Power 1945-1951*, Oxford University Press, 1984.
14. Mills, *The Power Elite*, and *The Causes of World War III*, London, Secker & Warburg, 1958.
15. Stuart Hall, *et al*, *Policing the Crisis*, London, Macmillan, 1978.
16. Anthony Barnett, *Iron Britannia*, London, Allison & Busby, 1982.

5

1. For the workers, James Hinton, *The First Shop Stewards Movement*, London, Allen and Unwin, 1973; on war-avoidance, Tony Ashworth, *Trench Warfare 1914-18: The Live and Let Live System*, London, Macmillan, 1981; on mutinies, Dallas and Gill, *The Unknown Army*.

2. See Walter Kendall, *The Revolutionary Movement in Britain 1900-21*, London, Weidenfeld & Nicolson, 1969; also the discussion in my 'Socialist internationalism, war and peace in Britain, 1895-1945' in Richard Taylor and Nigel Young, (eds.), *Campaigns for Peace*, Manchester University Press, 1988.

3. Ibid.

4. Kaldor, *The Baroque Arsenal*.

5. E.P. Thompson, *Beyond the Cold War*, London, Merlin/END, 1981.

6. See, for example, Ralph Miliband, 'The Politics of Peace and War' in M. Shaw (ed.), *War, State and Society*, pp. 119-35.

7. For an example – by no means the worst, but the more serious because it occurred in a tendency which seemed to offer some hope of avoiding this outcome – see the discussion of the forerunner of the British Socialist Workers Party in my 'The Making of a Party? The International Socialists 1965-76', *The Socialist Register 1978*, pp. 100-45.

8. Antonio Gramsci, *Selections from the Prison Notebooks*, London, Lawrence & Wishart, 1971.

9. Mills, *The Power Elite*.

10. Stuart Hall, 'Popular-Democratic *vs* Authoritarian Populism: Two Ways of "Taking Democracy Seriously"', in Alan Hunt (ed.), *Marxism and Democracy*, London, Lawrence & Wishart, 1981.

11. Hall *et al.*, *Policing the Crisis*.

12. Eric Hobsbawm in *Marxism Today*, March 1983.

13. See for example Thompson, *Beyond the Cold War*.

14. Peter Tatchell, *Democratic Defence*, London, Heretic/GMP, 1985.

15. For example, Alternative Defence Commission, *Defence without the Bomb*, London, Taylor & Francis, 1983.

16. E.P. Thompson, 'V.E. Day', *Sanity*, May 1985. Thompson does not, however, subscribe to a simple version of 'nuclear pacifism': see my discussion in 'From Total War to Democratic Peace: Exterminism and Historical Pacifism', in Harvey Kaye and Keith McClelland (eds.), *E.P. Thompson: Critical Debates*, Oxford, Polity, 1988.

Index